Charles Gavan Duffy and others

The Revival of Irish Literature

Charles Gavan Duffy and others

The Revival of Irish Literature

ISBN/EAN: 9783744716925

Printed in Europe, USA, Canada, Australia, Japan

Cover: Foto ©Thomas Meinert / pixelio.de

More available books at **www.hansebooks.com**

THE
REVIVAL OF IRISH LITERATURE
AND
OTHER ADDRESSES

THE REVIVAL OF IRISH LITERATURE

ADDRESSES BY SIR CHARLES GAVAN DUFFY, K.C.M.G., DR. GEORGE SIGERSON, AND DR. DOUGLAS HYDE

LONDON: T. FISHER UNWIN, PATERNOSTER SQUARE. MDCCCXCIV

CONTENTS.

The Revival of Irish Literature.

TWO ADDRESSES

DELIVERED BEFORE

THE IRISH LITERARY SOCIETY,

LONDON,

IN JULY, 1892, *AND JUNE*, 1893,

BY THE PRESIDENT,

The Hon. Sir CHARLES GAVAN DUFFY,

K.C.M.G.

WHAT IRISHMEN MAY DO FOR IRISH LITERATURE.

———◆———

SPEAKING to a Society of young Irishmen
who love their country and burn to serve
her, I am tempted to broach a subject which
has long lain in my mind, waiting for the fit
audience.

The famine of 1846 paralysed many forces
in Ireland, and none more disastrously than
our growing literature. How little has been
done in the region of mind since that calamity, and by what isolated and spasmodic
efforts? The era on which the famine fell
was intellectually a singularly fruitful one.
A group of young men, among the most
generous and disinterested in our annals,
were busy digging up the buried relics of
our history, to enlighten the present by a
knowledge of the past, setting up on their
pedestals anew the overthrown statues of

Irish worthies, assailing wrongs which under long impunity had become unquestioned and even venerable, and warming as with strong wine the heart of the people, by songs of valour and hope ; and happily not standing isolated in their pious work, but encouraged and sustained by just such an army of students and sympathisers as I see here to-day. The famine swept away their labours ; and their passionate attempts to arrest and redress the destruction which the famine inflicted, delivered them over to imprisonment and penal exile. Their incomplete work, produced amid the tumult and conflict of a great political struggle, has been a treasure to two generations of Irishmen ; and it supplied the impulse of work which rivalled their own. The publisher of Petrie's " Round Towers," and John O'Donovan's translation of " The Four Masters," assured me that he could not have ventured to issue books so costly, but for the enthusiasm kindled in the public mind by the young nationalists, and Butt and Lefanu, who at that time were strict Conservatives, confessed that while writing "The Gap of Barnesmore" and " The Cock and Anchor," they constantly thought

how welcome such works would be to Young
Irelanders. The patriot's library has not
been burthensome in latter times. But
Moore's melodies, Griffin's and Banim's novels,
the histories of MacGeoghegan and Curry,
and the writings of these young men have
been a constant cordial to the sorely-tried
spirit of our people. Since their day, individual writers have done useful work from
the unquenchable desire God has planted in
men's heart to serve their own race, but there
has been no organised attempt to raise the
mind of the country to higher and more
generous ideals of life and duty, or to quicken
its interest in things which it behoves us to
know. No nation can with impunity neglect
the mind of the growing generation, the
generation which after a little time will guide
its counsels and guard its interests. The
thought which has long haunted my reveries,
and which I desire to speak out to-day, is this—
that the young men of your generation might
and should take up anew the unfinished work
of their predecessors, and carry it another stage
towards the end which they aimed to reach.
Why should they not ? Every generation
of men furnishes its own tale of thinkers and

workers. The mind of Ireland has not grown barren, nor can I believe that it has grown indifferent, though public cares have diverted it away from intellectual pursuits. There are men, I do not doubt, fit and worthy and willing to undertake such a task.

Have you reflected on all we have lost, and are losing by the subsidence of the intellectual enthusiasm of half a century ago ? It is not alone that we are deficient in knowledge essential to equip us for the battle of life by an acquaintance with the character, capacities, and history of our own country ; but, far worse than that, the mind of the generation destined some day to fill our place, the youthful mind which used to be kindled and purified by the poetry and legends of Ireland, runs serious risks of becoming debased, perhaps depraved, by battening on literary garbage.

I have made inquiries, and I am assured that the books chiefly read by the young in Ireland are detective or other sensational stories from England and America, and vile translations from the French of vile originals. It is for the moralist, and indeed for all of us who love Ireland, to consider whether the virtues for which our people were distinguished, purity, piety, and simplicity, are not endangered by such intellectual diet. I have been vehemently warned that these detestable books can only be driven out by books more attractive, and I will not dispute the proposition. There are histories and biographies that delight the student, there is a poetry that is an inspiration and a solace to healthy minds, which it would be useless, I admit, to offer to young men accustomed to the dram-drinking of sensational literature. To them, at any rate, you must bring books which will excite and gratify the love of the wonderful, and carry them away from the commonplace world to regions of romance. And why may not this be done? Why may there not be opened to them a nobler world of wonder, the story of transcendent achievements, the romance of history, the " fairy tales of science " ? In the dominion of intellectual wonders there are many fair fields, and only one corner which is a stagnant fen. To the student, using that word in the wide sense which covers all who study, you must bring solider and more attractive offerings than the things you ask him to reject, and, again I ask, why should you not ?

It may be demanded : where are the writers to supply these captivating books ? Let me ask, Where, in 1840, were the writers who were exciting universal enthusiasm in 1843 ? Like them, the men of the future are consciously or unconsciously preparing for their task ; they are waiting the occasion—occasion which is the stage where alone great achievements are performed. I could name, if it were needful, a few writers not unworthy to succeed the men of '43, but their work will speak for them. I prefer to say that if there were not one man of genius left of the Irish race, there are already materials sufficient to furnish useful and delightful books for half-a-dozen years.

With a memory running back over six decades of reading, I confidently affirm that there are scattered in magazines and annuals, in luckless books neglected in the hurry of our political march, in publications the very names of which are forgotten by the present generation, Irish stories of surpassing interest, fit to win and fascinate young Irish readers, which would not degrade or debase them, but make them better men and better Irishmen. And in the other domains of intellect, Irish writers living in or belonging to a country where unhappily there was no market for books, carried their work to periodicals where it has lain interred for generations. How many rare and interesting books there are of which we have lost all trace and memory! I put lately into the hands of a friend of large intellectual appetite half-a-dozen little volumes of which he had never heard. "This," I said, pointing to the first, "was written by a Presbyterian minister, who describes with infinite humour the relations between the squire and the peasant a hundred years ago, and it is almost as true to-day as it was then. The writer was hanged as a rebel in '98 by the very squire whom he had depicted, but his little book is read with enthusiasm to this day by northern farmers who call themselves Orangemen and Unionists. This second volume, I said, is the first poem written by Bulwer Lytton, and the hero is an O'Neill who rallied his nation against England. Here's a brochure on the Land Question, published in America fifty years ago by a poor exiled Irishman, which anticipates the alarming proclamation of first principles by Fintan Lalor and Henry George, and it is as unknown in Ireland as the lost books of Livy." I do not suggest that you should publish these books or any of them, but surely they are finger-posts pointing to an unexplored territory. While I am speaking of the resources for a popular library, which we have in hand, I may say that one-third of the writings of Thomas Davis or Clarence Mangan has not been collected in volumes. Davis's most remarkable achievement as an historian, "The Patriot Parliament" he calls it—not the Parliament of Grattan, but the Parliament of Tyrconnell, was prepared ɩfor publication by his own hand, and it has remained without a publisher for two generations. Nothing of the miscellaneous writings of John Blake Dillon, John O'Hagan, Thomas Meagher, or Charles Kickham, have been gathered into books. And how much of the wealth of our ancient Gaelic literature still lies buried in untranslated MSS., or in the transactions of learned societies.

A perfectly honest and respectable blockhead asked me recently, "What is the use of books for men working for their daily bread, or for young fellows whose first business in life is to make some way in the world?" From the highest class in the nation to the

humblest, good books are the salt of life. They
make us wiser, manlier, more honest, and
what is less than any of these, more prosperous.
It is not the least of their merits that good
books make manly men and patriotic citizens.
Robert Burns declared that reading the " Life
of William Wallace " poured a tide of Scottish
sentiment into his veins, which would boil till
the flood-gates of life shut in eternal rest. A
man who has done and suffered much for
Ireland during the last forty years, has often
avowed that he was made a patriot by reading
the Poems of Thomas Davis ; and how many
other Irishmen have confessed the same debt
to him and his associates ? The great
Dominican, Father Burke, and Professor
Tyndall of Belfast, the fierce Unionist, are
equally warm in their acknowledgment of
the effect produced upon them in their youth
by the writings of the Young Irelanders. The
late Judge O'Hagan, one of the most upright
and gifted of Irishmen, used to declare that
the evening when he first read the address
of John Blake Dillon to the College Historical Society, he was a Whig, but the next
day, and ever after, he was a Nationalist. To
how many of us is that Address still in-

accessible ? Would it not be a beneficent work to republish it ? Surely there is no Irishman of any political persuasion who would not welcome the opportunity of reading a work which produced such an effect on such a man.

But the discipline of education is not for ornament merely, but for practical use. Without it men and nations miss their path in life, and see not at all, or only with purblind eyes, open roads to national prosperity. In Australia I have known a generation of shepherds and sheep-farmers, who long trod a soil seamed with gold, knowing nothing of the treasures beneath their feet. Is not the Irish farmer often as ignorant of the wealth which other nations draw from the earth, or from the enterprise born of the leisure and security which the possession of the soil creates ? The domestic industries which help to make French farms prosperous are just as suitable to our own country, and just as feasible in it. London is supplied from Normandy with farm produce which would come more naturally from Munster, and the French make their households pleasant with dainty preparations of vegetables which the

Irish fling away with contempt ; Switzerland is more destitute of coal than Ireland, but Switzerland competes successfully with England in her own markets with manufactures for which she does not possess even the raw material. When I met in France, Italy, and Egypt the marmalade manufactured at Dundee, I felt it like a silent reproach. Oranges do not grow in Dundee, and sugar is not manufactured there, but enterprise and industrial education are native to the soil. Is not this a department in which there is something to be taught to the people by useful books ? Ideas are the root of action, and books are the cabinets of ideas. If work of a practical and patriotic spirit is to be done in any country, books must be the beginning of that work ; and why should we not have such books ?

What do we hope to make of Ireland ?— this is the fundamental question on which the character of education ought to depend. In Switzerland the bulk of the people live on their own farms, not needing or desiring great wealth, but enjoying free, simple lives, ennobled by the perfect liberty which the poet declares is a child of the mountains. In Belgium there are many husbandmen thriving on the benign industries cultivated at home, which rear a nobler class of men than the stricken legions who serve the steam-engine and the water-wheel. It is not for me to dogmatise on the proper development of Ireland, but assuredly to be wise and successful it must harmonise with the nature of the people, and correct it where correction is needful. Education is far stronger than nature, and there is no doubt the deficiencies in national character may be repaired by discipline. The highest teaching of a people is to accustom them to have a strict regard for the rights of others, to be prudent and temperate in action, and to regard the whole nation as members of a common household. To make our people politically free, yet leave them bond-slaves of some debasing social system like that which crowds the mines and factories of England with squalid victims, or make the artisans of France so often godless scoffers, would be a poor result of all Ireland's labours and sacrifices.

Liberty will do much for a nation, but it will not do everything. Among a people who do not know and reverence their own ancestors, who do not submit cheerfully to lawful authority, and do not love the eternal principles of justice, it will do little. But moral sentiments, generous impulses, religious feelings still survive in the Irish race, and they give assurance that in that mystic clime on the verge of the Western Ocean, where the more debasing currents of European civilisation only reach it at high tide, there is place for a great experiment for humanity. There within our circling seas we may rear a race in which the fine qualities of the Celtic family, fortified by the sterner strength of the North, and disciplined by the Norman genius of Munster may at last have fair play ; where, at lowest a pious and gallant race may after long struggles and nameless sufferings possess their own soil and their own souls in peace.

Let me say, though I have said it more than once before, that the Celts are among the most teachable of races. The drill, the jacket, the discipline, transform an Irish peasant into a sub-constable with almost as military a carriage, and as expert an eye and hand as a veteran of the Peninsula. A few years in a National School, and the boy who emerged from a smoky and squalid cabin, shared with a pig, is turned into a clean and shapely youth, fit to wrestle with the world, and perhaps to win the match. Look at a railway porter, or a railway policeman—the decent uniform and the punctual system soon make a new man of the peasant. An English priest in Paris, with little prejudice in favour of our race, assured me that no girls crossed the sea who acquire so speedily the carriage, deportment, and grace which distinguish French women, as girls from Munster, coming perhaps as servants to some great lady. And this physical training is a small achievement compared with the result of discipline on the *intellect* and *practical power* of cultivated, aspiring men. The one multiplies iron, the other multiplies rarest gold of Ophir. But we have not, I fear, made even a beginning in the practical education which makes industry prosperous. I lived for a quarter of a century in Australia, and there rarely came an English ship into the port of Melbourne that did not bring me letters of introduction with young Irishmen who hoped to make their home in the new country. Such of them as it was possible to place in the public service, and that was a limited number, did their work extremely well. But after I had done all that

I reasonably could do—for I was administering the affairs of a colony where three-fourths of the inhabitants were English and Scotch, and the patronage had to be distributed in just relation to the population—an enormous remnant remained to be provided for. Some of them were as bright, intelligent young fellows as I ever met in the world, but they were wholly untrained in any business. They had no profession and no trade ; they were merely nice fellows, and agreeable idle gentlemen. Now what became of them in the new country, where there was work and pay for everybody who was willing and able to work, and brought to the public service some capacity worth paying for ? Multitudes of them sank to be waiters in hotels, barbers, and cabmen. The man who had a trade prospered in a wonderful manner, the man who had a profession prospered, according to his capacity, but the man who was ready " to do anything " generally found nothing to do.

It has been asked scornfully what we can hope to effect in a little country with diminishing population and limited resources ? Ought not some Irish student to teach our people that it is not great states like those which the greed of conquerors has aggregated, but states scarcely larger than an Irish province which have done the most memorable work for humanity and civilisation? The achievements in arts, arms, science, and discovery, and in the art of government of the Greek Republics, of the Italian Republics, of the trampled provinces of Spain in the Low Countries, of the little rib taken out of the side of Spain, and called Portugal, how emphatically they teach the lesson that it is not by the quantity but by the quality of their men that states are glorified ! A little book which told this great story would be a boon to our people.

It would be presumptuous to name the books which ought to be published in such an enterprise, but we may profitably consider the class and character to be preferred.

Big books of history are only for students, they are never read by the people. But they will read picturesque biographies, which are history individualised, or vivid sketches of memorable eras, which are history vitalised. A dozen lives of representative Irishmen would teach more of the training and growth of Ireland than a library of annals and State papers. They would familiarise us with great men, whom the Celt loves better than systems or policies. This is the class of books in which we are most deficient ; there is no memoir of Roger O'Moore, none of Luke Wadding, none of Patrick Sarsfield, none of a man as fertile in intellect, as firm in judgment as any of these, a man whom some of us have seen in the flesh, the wise and fearless J. K. L. Mr. Fitzpatrick has collected his letters and literary remains with commendable care, it only needs that some sympathetic student should ponder over them till the electric spark is kindled, that a new figure may be given to our imagination for ever. The first great poet who sang the wrongs of Ireland with civilised Europe for an audience, has never had an adequate memoir. He has been singularly unfortunate in his biographer ; Lord John Russell discharged on the public several cart-loads of undigested diaries as " The Memoirs and Journals of Thomas Moore." They are of little use to anybody at present, but a skilful literary workman, or a chemist of the intellect, could extract a delightful little volume from the chaotic mass.

How profitable it would be if the best men

of this time would contribute each of them a study to a gallery of representative Irishmen ! We are accustomed to say, with not unjust reproach, that England knows little of our country ; but, alas ! my friends, we Irishmen know too little of it ourselves. 'Tis a great possession given to us by a gracious God, which we do not take adequate pains to comprehend ; and the philosopher has declared with profound truth that men only possess what they understand.

And we want works reproduced which have disappeared out of circulation. The hundred best Irish books have been skilfully discussed in the newspapers, but the young student soon discovers that half of the hundred are out of print, or locked up in costly editions. Fifty pounds would not purchase the volumes recommended. But it would not be impossible to produce a library containing these very books, or a collection varied by admitting some books more pertinent to our present wants, for fifty shillings, to be paid over a period of three or four years — an expenditure which would be burthensome to few Irishmen accustomed to read.

How are the good books to be circulated

effectually? I have always insisted, and I do now emphatically insist that if this thing is to be well done the young men of Irish birth at home and abroad must regard it as their work, and be determined it shall succeed. They must supply canvassers in every centre of Irish feeling in Ireland, England, Scotland, America, and Australia. And where the young men are still struggling for a foothold in the world, the work ought not to be made burthensome to them, but reproductive. There exists in America a system of canvassing agents by which books are brought to the remotest farmhouses, and the canvassers paid a reasonable compensation. Ought we not to imitate this method in our enterprise?

It will be our duty to see that the literary labourers also shall be fairly paid, for they are commonly neither a sordid nor even a provident race. It will be a labour of love to them to feed the mind of their country, as it has been a labour of love to the men of their class everywhere. Who can read without a glow of sympathy how the struggling Scotch farmer and exciseman who gave immortal songs to Scotland, refused pecuniary reward for a work which he desired to be one of pure patriotism;

or how the indigent French poet, living contentedly in an humble Pension in the Champs Elysees, on an annuity from his publisher, declined a seat in the Chamber of Deputies from the Republic which he had done so much to make possible, and still more emphatically declined all aid or recognition from the Bonaparte family, to whose cause he had recalled the French nation by splendid but too indiscriminate panegyrics on its founder ; or how our own national poet, who alone in modern times is fit to be named with the other two as a writer of songs that will live for ever, rejected in turn a national tribute, a seat in Parliament, and the assistance of opulent friends under unexpected calamity — Moore, like Burns and Beranger, being determined that the purity of his devotion to his country should run no risk of being misunderstood ?

Wherever there is an Irish bookseller, at home or in the two new worlds, who has taken an intelligent, not merely a sordid interest in his business, he is the natural agent of this design ; and in the many districts where there is no bookseller at present a *quasi* bookseller might be created. If the popular journals in Dublin encourage their agents to act on behalf of the enterprize, a solid body of retail dealers would be at once available. I have spoken only of Irish readers, our duty begins with them, but it does not end with them. Ireland has many friends in England, and good books have friends everywhere. The volumes of such a Library ought to be found on the bookstalls from Liverpool to Edinburgh, they ought to be proffered to the passengers by the great transatlantic routes, and to the eager crowd of purchasers who throng the book arcades of Melbourne and Sydney. Can all this be done? Who will be our Minister of Public Instruction, to organise it and set it in motion? If there be such a one, I think I see here many who will be his willing associates and assistants. For one old man who can only hope to see the good work fairly begun, I can promise that whatever he can do with his moderate resources to help it in money, or with his waning powers to help it with cordial co-operation, shall not be wanting.

If we can revive the love of noble books among our people, that is a result which standing alone is worth striving for. To love noble books is to share with statesmen and philosophers the pleasure on which they set the highest price. Time has made trite and commonplace the great saying of Fénélon, "If the crowns of Europe were laid at my feet in exchange for books and the love of reading, I would spurn them all." Our own Goldsmith declares that taking up a new book worth reading is like making a new friend ; a friend from whom we will never be separated by any of the melancholy mischances on which human friendships are so often wrecked. But good books will do more than this—they will awaken all that is best in our nature, and teach us to live worthier lives. They will do for us what we rarely permit the closest friend to do—they will teach us our faults and how to amend them. What they might do, not for the individual, but for the nation, I dare not predict—the possibilities are so prodigious. One of the keenest intellects of the eighteenth century declared that the world was ruled by books. What, think you, has most profoundly altered the condition of the world in the last hundred years? Kings, statesmen, conquerors? Not so ; an armful of books, about as many as a schoolboy carries in his satchel. The result of these books was not always beneficent, but it was always immense. The war of arms and of diplomacy which England carried on against the French Republic and the French Empire for a dozen years, and which left us the National Debt as a memorial, took its first impulse from a little book written by Edmund Burke. The Revolution which it combatted was as certainly the fruit of other books. The declaration of Irish independence pronounced by the Convention at Dunganon, and confirmed by the parliament in College Green, simply formulated the doctrine of a little volume by Molyneux which the House of Commons at Westminster had caused to be burned by the common hangman. All that has been done in later days for Free Trade and unrestricted competition, for the self-government of Colonies, and the education of the people, was first taught in the treatise of an Edinburgh professor ; a book which has influenced the current of thought and legislation in the British Empire, and far beyond it, more than any other book written since the invention of printing.[1] The desire to unfetter the negro which culminated in the decrees of Abraham Lincoln and the victories of Ulysses Grant

[1] Adam Smith's " Wealth of Nations."

began in a work of genius written by a woman and read by the whole civilized world. The successive despots expelled during the last sixty years by the French people, from Charles the Tenth to Napoleon the Third, were driven out less at the point of the bayonet than at the point of the pen. The social changes wrought by books in the same era we would, perhaps, relinquish less willingly than any of these political gains. The humanising of English law long steeped in blood and tears, is less attributable to bench and bar than to the books of Jeremy Bentham. If the Court of Chancery is no longer the patron and factor of dilapidated edifices and ruined fortunes, if the Dotheboys halls of Yorkshire are shut up, is it not chiefly to a couple of novels by Charles Dickens we owe these salutary changes? One little volume written by a woman, critics assure us, routed filth and laziness out of the farmhouses of Scotland. It was the novelist Charles Reade who made Englishmen ashamed of the murderous silent system in prisons, and it was he and another novelist who put an end (for I hope the end has come) to the shameful abuses of private lunatic asylums. And it was only the other day that, by a little domestic story, Walter Besant, with the magic wand of art, raised a Palace of Delight, where the labouring poor find refreshment and culture in the dreary desert of East London—so fertilising and fruitful are good books.

Our books may not achieve any of these marvels, but there are results not beyond their reach. England holds the sympathies of all the communities which share her blood, less by obeying the same laws than by loving the same books. And if we do not fail in our task the volumes of the Irish Library will be read by the Irish settler in Canada, the Irish digger in California and Australia, our missionaries and soldiers in India, the adventurous pioneer in Africa, the exile far away in Florida, in Michigan, in Egypt, or in Siam, with more love and enthusiasm than even in the homesteads of Leinster and Munster.

BOOKS FOR THE IRISH PEOPLE.

It is nearly a year since I opened to this Society the design of inducing young Irishmen of the present generation to take up anew a task which famine and political disaster interrupted among their predecessors — the task of teaching the Irish people to understand their own country. The Irish people have never ceased to love their country, they have never shrunk from any labour or sacrifice to serve her, but they do not understand Ireland as the Swiss understand Switzerland ; as the Flemings understand the sandbank which their industry has turned into a model farm ; or as the Venetians understand the primitive quagmire which Italian genius transformed into one of the wonders, of the world.

A year may seem a long time to have employed in preliminary arrangements ; but it
was not wasted. There were many difficulties
to overcome and they have been overcome.
We are now in a position to announce that
our first volume is printed, and ready to be
issued, that the second volume is in the
printer's hands, and successive volumes for
more than a year are in preparation. I may
mention that the original design of acting
through a Limited Liability Company was
abandoned in favour of a better plan ; a successful and experienced publisher, Mr. Fisher
Unwin, takes the responsibility of producing
the books, leaving the men of letters to the
task for which they are fitter, that of devising
and writing them.

The new Irish Library will be offered to all
who desire to welcome it, in New York and
Melbourne and the continents to which they
belong, as well as in Dublin and London ;
and we hope by an organised system of col-
portage to carry the books to many districts
where there are no regular booksellers at
present, or no market for Irish books.

When I say we do not understand Ireland,
I do not mean merely that we are imperfectly

acquainted with its history, its literature, its art, and its memorable men ; but which of us studies Irish statistics till he understands them as he does a current account with a tradesman or a banker ? Which of us studies the topography, the political and commercial geography, the botany, the geology, the resources and deficiencies of the country so as to qualify him to handle its interests, in a parish or a parliament, if that task should present itself ?

The prosperous wiseacre whom the Germans call a Philistine, and the French an *épicier*, will tell you that study does not pay. But that respectable citizen may be assured that whatever he values most in his narrow life, whatever adds to its comfort and convenience, whatever simplifies and facilitates his beloved trade (of which steam and electricity are the nerves and sinews) is nothing else than the remote result of some student's midnight toil. The garments he wears, the furniture of his trim home, not less than the laws which protect his life and the customs which render it easy and pleasant, even the ideas grown commonplace by time which he daily thinks he is thinking, were discovered, invented, or brought from regions more civilised, by men whose toil he undervalues; and if all he owes to study and the intellectual enterprise it begets were snatched away, his home would be almost as naked as the Redman's wigwam. But if the man of business be moreover a man of meditation and culture, he and his class are among the most indispensable forces of a nation, for it is such men who turn the student's airy speculation into accomplished fact.

Of all studies that one which a nation can least safely dispense with is a study of its own history. Some one has invented the audacious axiom that history never repeats itself, but it would be truer to affirm that history is always repeating itself ; assuredly in our own history identical weaknesses and identical virtues recur from generation to generation, and to know them may teach us where weak places in national and individual character need to be fortified and strong ones developed.

Of politics, if it were only the politics of a parish, what can we know worth knowing unless the lamp of history lights the misty way ? And the great problem of all—for

what special career do the gifts and deficiencies
of our race, their position on the globe, their
past and their present career best fit them ?—
only a familiarity with their annals will
enable any one to say.

Another use of historical study is to enable
us to vindicate our race from unjust asper-
sions. This is no sentimental gain, but one
eminently practical ; Ireland and Irishmen
suffer wrong from systematic misrepresenta-
tion, which only better knowledge will cure.
Which of us has not heard mimics of Macaulay
disparaging the Irish Parliament of James II.
as a disgrace to civilisation, or Mr. Froude's
gloomy devotees lift their hands in horror at
the Rising of 1641 ? We purpose to face
these calumnies. In the first volume of our
series, Thomas Davis, reprinting the principal
Acts of James' Parliament, criticises them in
careful detail, and finds them for the most
part just, moderate, and generous. Whoever
takes up the story of 1641, in the same
judicial spirit cannot fail to pronounce that
though in the end barbarities were committed
on both sides of that struggle, according to
the evil habit of the age throughout Europe,
the original design of the old inhabitants to

repossess themselves of lands taken from them
by fraud and violence a generation earlier, was
a design which the twelve apostles might have
sanctioned. I read quiet recently, with a good
deal of surprise, a new reproach to Irishmen,
derived from the history of the last century.
It was not Celts, we are told, but Normans
and Saxons, who served the Empire with dis-
tinction a century ago in peace and war.
Marvellous fact, indeed, that the Catholic
Celt did not distinguish himself as a statesman or a general when he was peremptorily
shut out by law from the Senate and the
Council of War, and that he did not make
scientific and practical discoveries when he
was deliberately denied education. But history will teach us that wherever there was
an open door, as on the Continent and in
the New World beyond the Atlantic, and in
later times in all the Colonies of the Empire,
the Celt has done notable work, and never in
a solitary instance been unfaithful to the trust
so tardily and so reluctantly confided to him.
These mordant critics would exalt the men of
English descent by disparaging the men of
Celtic breed, but in vain. We regard all
Irishmen who love their country, whatever

be their creed or pedigree, as equally our countrymen. We rejoice in the splendid record of success in arms, arts, literature, and diplomacy which the Irish minority can exhibit ; we acknowledge thankfully that wherever the rank of native patriots became thin or broken, men of the other race leaped into their perilous places ; and we cannot look on the noble edifices which adorn the Irish capital, two of them not excelled by the Palace of Legislation or the Palace of Commerce in any capital of Europe, without thankfully remembering how much our country owes to the cultivated genius of the minority. If the races who inhabit these islands are ever to understand and honour each other, it must be on condition of comprehending the past, not hiding it away ; and history is the reservoir from which such knowledge is drawn.

I know no civilised country, except Ireland, whose history is not familiar to its people. In England you encounter English history everywhere ; in literature, in art, on the stage, and even in the pulpit. In France, not merely endless books, but museums and picture galleries are devoted to the illustration of French history. In the United States the schoolboy is taught the principles of the American constitution as part of the regular curriculum. Even in Australia its brief history of a single century has been made a school-book in State schools ; but in Ireland the national history is never named in the schools called national, and that it may be known vólunteers must attempt the task which the State has neglected and forbidden.

If the statesman gladly acknowledges that such intellectual discipline makes men better citizens, the moralist rejoices to know that it makes them better men. I can confidently affirm, for I have seen the prodigy wrought, that strenuous self-discipline, with love of country for its inspiration, burns up the grosser sentiments in young men, and teaches them that life has happier as well as nobler pursuits than self-indulgence ; teaches them to abjure sensual and slavish vices, and warm their souls with the divine flame of patriotism. An Irish poet has named the teacher "God's second priest," and a great ecclesiastic, who was also a wise guide in mundane affairs, the illustrious J. K. L. declared more than half a century ago that religion could not dispense with this potent auxiliary.

Religion herself," he said, "loses her beauty and influence when not attended by education; and her power, splendour, and majesty are never so exalted as when cultivated genius and refined taste become her heralds and her handmaids. Many have become fools for Christ, and by their simplicity and piety have exalted the glory of the Cross; but Paul, not John, was the Apostle of the Nations; and doctors, even more than prophets, have been sent to declare the truth before kings and princes, and the nations of the earth."

One of the worst defects in our course of discipline in and out of school (for a young man gives himself his most effectual education after he has escaped from the hands of the schoolmaster) is that it is rarely practical. We learn little thoroughly, and little of a useful and reproductive character, and we commonly pay the penalty in a lower place in the world. As far as I am able to judge Scotsmen are not gifted by nature with qualities superior to those of Irishmen, but in more than one country I have seen Irishmen performing some of the roughest and most menial offices in gangs directed by Scotch overseers. And why? No intelligent man has any doubt of the cause. For nearly two centuries Scotland has had excellent parish schools, where the children of the industrious

population get a practical and religious education at the cost of the State. In Dublin I
have seen two of the most national institutions in the country, a great Irish journal and
a great Irish publishing house, managed by
Scotsmen. Again why? For no intelligible
reason except that the Scotch boy is taught
mathematics and trained early in business.
This defect, like so many of our shortcomings,
has an origin which we must search for in
history. Till 1833 there were no public
schools in Ireland which were not openly
designed to proselytise the people, and since
there have been neutral schools, the principal
condition of their existence has been the
exclusion from their teaching of the history
and religion of the people. I remember Mr.
Bright saying to me during some temporary
repulse of the North in the American Civil
War: "Be assured the end is not at all
doubtful ; the States which have had three
generations of solid education must win
against a mob of arrogant self-indulgent
slave-drivers." I felt bitterly that the con-
verse of the axiom might be applied to our
own country. And if we look into the
matter the happiness and independence of

nations seem everywhere to bear a strict proportion to their moral and intellectual training. Switzerland spends as much money on education as on soldiers and their costly equipment ; Denmark half as much, and Belgium about a third, and these are all prosperous and contented little States. But the great empires which clutch territory and ignore men, spend prodigally on their armies and parsimoniously on their people. In Prussia education obtains scarcely a fifth of the amount lavished on preparations for war ; in England only one-sixth the amount ; in Italy less than a tenth ; and in Russia a hundred pounds are squandered on turning peasants into soldiers for every twenty shillings spent on making the peasants fitter to perform their duties in the world. For my part I would rather see our people developed according to their special gifts than see them masters of limitless territory or inexhaustible gold reefs. A Celtic people trained to become all that their nature fits them to be—humane, joyous, and generous, living diligent, tranquil lives in their own land, and sending out from time to time, as of old, men whose gifts and faculties fitted them to become benefactors of mankind—that is the destiny I desire for my country. None of us can be ignorant of the fact that a change has come over the national character in latter times which is not altogether a change for the better. The people are more alert and resolute than of old, and that is well; but they are more gloomy and resentful, and something of the piety and simplicity of old seems to have disappeared. Nature made them blithe, frank, and hospitable; pleasant comrades and trusty friends; but hard laws and hard taskmasters have sometimes perverted their native disposition. To my thinking that patient, long-suffering, bitterly wronged people still preserve fresh and perennial many of the spiritual endowments which are among the greatest possessions of a nation. But, like soldiers returning from a long campaign, who bring back something of the manners and *morale* of the camp, twenty years of agitation, which however just and necessary was inevitably demoralising, has blunted their moral sensibility. Blessed be those who will warn them that to be just and considerate towards friends and opponents, to refrain from cruelty or wrong under any temptation, and to speak and act and applaud only the rigid truth, are the practices which make nations honoured and happy.

What writers ought to aim at, who hope to benefit the people, is to fill up the blanks which an imperfect education, and the fever of a tempestuous time, have left in their knowledge, so that their lives might become contented and fruitful. Let me take an instance—I have sometimes marvelled that no one has made it his special task to teach the "tenants at will," who have become proprietors under the Land Purchase Act, what wonders they may accomplish for themselves and the country. To become prosperous and independent by systematic industry is not the greatest of their opportunities ; by liberal education and healthy spiritualised lives, spent on the paternal estate, they may make their sons and daughters types of whatever is best in the Celtic character. But they have much to learn and few to teach them. In the United States there is a public department whose business is to furnish settlers on the public lands with the latest information on agricultural science, and with a supply of suitable seeds for new experiments. In the

Colonies they are helped also, though less effectually I think. In Ireland scarcely any one has given them so much as good advice or good wishes. I hope some one will write in the new Irish Library a book for this class, describing the *petites cultures*, and the localised industries of the Continent and the honest outdoor enjoyments which help to make life happy. Why may these men not realise the dream of the poet of what Irish farmers, free from feudal bonds, might become ?

" The Happy Land,
    Studded with cheerful homesteads fair to see,
    With garden grace and household symmetry ;
    How grand the wide-brow'd peasant's lordly mien
    The matron's smile serene !
          O happy, happy land ! "

I have refrained from specifying books which might be written, and books which ought to be republished, because a design is fatally discounted by promising too much at the outset. It is perhaps enough to say that they must be issued at a price which the people can afford to pay, or they will not buy them ; and they must interest them, or they

will not read them, though they got them for
nothing. Although it is an essential basis of
the enterprise to publish books useful to the
people, that is not enough. If you would
drive out the impure and atheistical but
sensational literature borrowed from the
French, you must replace it by stimulating
stories of our own land ; and it will not be
safe to neglect poetry, for as a recent poet
sings—

"Dear to the Gael 's the clash of swords,
And dear the ring of rhyme."

The editors will not print anything which
they do not believe useful and beneficial,
but they must not be held responsible for
every sentence and sentiment in books origi-
nated, or reprinted, under their direction. A
too rigid strictness might involve an amount
of alteration, which would be fair neither to
the author nor the reader, and would be fatal
to the generous and liberal freedom in which
alone literature thrives. I will only add that
if the Irish people second our design cordially,
the stream which will now begin to flow shall
not soon run dry. But remember that success

depends mainly on you and your compeers.
What is the use of writing books if they are
not read and pondered on, and their lessons
taken to heart? Without a sympathetic
audience the orator is only a lay figure,
without a sympathetic circle of readers the
writer is a wasted force. We labour for the
young men and young women of Ireland, on
whom the future of our race depends; and
our hope is that they may respond as cordially
as their predecessors did fifty years ago; that
they may aim to gain a complete knowledge
of their own country, and come forth from
the study steeped in Irish memories, proud
of Irish traditions, panting with Irish hopes.
Every Irishman, anywhere in the world, who
wishes well to our design, can help it a little;
but there is one class whose good wishes are
indispensable. Father Hogan, a professor
of Maynooth College, has appealed to his
brethren in the ministry, in language which
I prefer to any I could employ on the subject :—

"None like the working clergy (he says) can realise
the baneful effects that are produced by pernicious books,
and how fatal to the innocence of youth, and to the
strength of national as well as of personal character, they

so often prove. There are none, moreover, who have the same responsibility cast upon them to oppose the current of evil, and to maintain at the same time the noble and traditional generosity of the Church towards literature and men of letters. Our denunciations of dangerous books, and especially of light and licentious reading, would be justly regarded as mere empty sound were we unwilling to lend a helping hand to a movement, the chief object of which is to stir up and encourage amongst the young men of Ireland a wholesome desire for what is good, and a salutary contempt for what is either silly or debased."

There is another class whose help we cannot spare—Irish journalists in Ireland, England, America, and Australia. They can make our undertaking known to all who read, and can drop the same thought, as de Tocqueville says, into a thousand minds at the same moment. They have helped us hitherto, and they will help us for the future, I make no doubt, as far as we deserve help, and we are entitled to expect no more.

It will be a pleasant task hereafter, I trust, to remember some of the dismal predictions which our enterprise had to encounter at the outset. The black prophets, who believe in no good till it is accomplished, warned us that we labour in vain, that our population is yearly decreasing, and is destined to merge in an imperial race, whose voice may be heard uttering the word of command in the five great divisions of the world, and that the men who remain are broken by quarrels as old as tradition, and never likely to end. I would like to conclude with a word on each of these objections. It is true we are united to a race who dominate huge tracts of the globe, but I have visited four of the five great divisions in question, and I can affirm that the word of command is not unfrequently uttered with an Ulster burr, or an unequivocal Munster brogue. In every great colony it has been spoken from the *dais* of authority in the accents we love. Nay, more, I met officers in the service of France and Belgium, and some who had served in Austria, indistinguishable from Frenchmen and Germans in their ordinary conversation, who, when they strayed into English, became unmistakably Leinster-men or Munster-men, but none of these Irishmen show the least disposition to merge themselves in any other race. And the millions of our people in America, are they not more Irish than the Irish at home? No, there is no danger that we shall lose

our nationality, or weary of labouring for
it.

"The toil for Ireland once begun,
We never will give o'er,
Nor own a land on earth but one—
We're Paddies evermore."

It is too true that our population is still
diminishing ; generations must perhaps pass
before it regains the maximum it had reached
fifty years ago ; but let not that disastrous
fact discourage us overmuch. It is not by
the number, but by the intrinsic value of its
men and women that a country becomes
powerful and memorable. The true ad-
measurement, as we may learn from the
inspiring story of small nations, is not geo-
metrical but metaphysical. Little Athens
gave philosophy, literature, and art to mankind ; little Rome imposed her will on all the
peoples of the known world ; in modern times
little Portugal, with a population which sometimes fell short of the population of Munster,
undertook great enterprises, made memorable
discoveries of new territory, and established
in Asia and Africa settlements, which, after
troubled centuries, still survive. The little
Netherlands, with no more men than Portu-

gal, held its own against the most powerful
monarchy in Europe, and planted new
Netherlands in distant countries. Florence
almost alone created and fostered the Renais-
sance which after desolate ages

> "———— blessed mankind
> With arts anew, and civilised the world."

But these are the commonplaces of history,
compared to the story of the single city of
Italy, which, with one arm, "held the golden
East in fee," and with the other drove back
the conquering Turk, bent on the destruction
of Christendom. Or, for an example, that not
men but mind is the conquering force, turn to
the barren mountains of Switzerland, where
free institutions were first planted by a hand-
ful of husbandmen and hunters, less than
occupy one Irish county, and to-day a fede-
rated league of two and twenty separate
republics enjoy substantial prosperity and
ideal liberty, though they muster fewer men
than still occupy the two side of the Boyne.
No ; trust me, you have men enough, if they
be endowed with the gifts and disciplined
by the culture, which make the destiny of
nations.

It would be vain to deny that national quarrels are the most intractable of our troubles. The Celt is placable and generous in private transactions, but for public conflicts he has an unsleeping memory. Some of these quarrels are nearly as old as the Flood. The late Martin Haverty, who wrote a meritorious history of Ireland, was once discovered by a friend in a perturbed and angry mood, which he explained by the fact that he had been reading a record of ill-usage his ancestors sustained from the invaders. "The slaughter of the Milesians by Strongbow?" queried his friend. "No," said the historian, "I speak of the slaughter inflicted by the villanous Milesians on my ancestors the Tuatha De Danaans." No one can tell with certainty the date of that transaction within a thousand years or so, and it might perhaps be permitted to rest in peace. There is another Irish historian and poet, who represents a race to which we have not yet got altogether reconciled. Our friend, Dr. Sigerson, is as unmitigated a Dane as the great soldier from whom his name is derived. When I was last in Dublin I proposed a final burial of national feuds, ancient and modern, and, as a last victim might be required to consecrate the transaction, I suggested, that we might execute this last Dane on the field of Clontarf, where, by some unaccountable mischance, his ancestor escaped the conquering sword of Bryan. The Doctor offered no objection to so reasonable a proposal, but suggested that the tramway from Nelson's Pillar to Clontarf should run quarter-hour trains on the day of execution, as he wanted a large audience to tell them what they certainly did not know, that there was a strong Danish contingent in Bryan's Irish army, and that the Danes, so far from being exterminated at Clontarf, maintained themselves in Ireland for many generations afterwards, and still constitute a solid element in our population. Some clement person suggested that as the sons and daughters of Siger are among the most gifted patriots in the country just now, it might be discreet to forgive them offences nearly ten centuries old, but he was pronounced out of order. I am rejoiced to say a compromise was arrived at in the end, by which, if the learned doctor will undertake to translate some of the most characteristic of the Scandanavian sagas for the new Irish Library, and make us better acquainted generally with the Norse literature, so far as it relates to Ireland, his punishment may be postponed, and perhaps altogether remitted. There is another nation with whom our quarrels are more recent, more bitter, and more prolonged, but it would be genuine wisdom to make peace with them also if they will let us. The memory of wrongs which are perpetuated and renewed cannot be forgotten ; but, while no man knows better than I do how just are our complaints and how terrible the memories they evoke, I affirm that the best Irishmen are prepared *toto corde* to forget and forgive the past, if its policy and practices are never to reappear. The Rules of this Society forbid me to speak of later quarrels, whether international or internecine ; but surely no people ever were more emphatically exhorted by the circumstances in which they stand, to close their ranks and end their feuds. Our efforts in this Society will, I trust, contribute to promote that end.

I have spoken only of the revival of literature for the people, for happily there has never been altogether wanting a literature for the studious and thoughtful; maintained by the spontaneous zeal of a few gifted men

and women. It slept at times, but only for
an interval. O'Conor and Curry, Miss Edge-
worth and Lady Morgan, Banim and Griffin,
have had successors down to our own day
when we are still at times delighted with
glowing historic or legendary stories, or
charming idylls of the people, bright and
natural as a bunch of shamrocks with the
dew of Munster fresh upon them. One
secluded scholar has spent his manhood col-
lecting our national records with a care and
zeal which in any other country would com-
pel the recognition and reward of the State ;
a group of scholars not connected, I think,
except by the *camaraderie* of a kindred
pursuit, have created a great revival in Gaelic
literature ; and the Irish press has not for a
generation devoted so much thought to native
literature and art, national customs and
manners, as it does just now. There are still
local periodicals full of the enthusiasm of old
for our national antiquities, and it is pleasant
to know that they are often sustained by men
who differ from the majority in race, creed,
and political opinions. I rarely see without a
strong sentiment of affection and sympathy a
little sixpenny magazine conducted for twenty

years by the zeal of one solitary priest who watches like a father over whatever concerns the Irish intellect. It is good, therefore, to know that we are not sailing against wind and tide. The spirit of the era, the state of men's minds as well as the manifest need of such an enterprise are favourable to our experiment, and I trust it shall not fail by any indolence or apathy of those who have taken the responsibility of initiating it.

If I were to express in one phrase the aim of this Society, and of kindred societies, and of the literary revival of which I have been speaking, it is to begin another deliberate attempt to make of our Celtic people all they are fit to become—to increase knowledge among them, and lay its foundations deep and sure ; to strengthen their convictions and enlarge their horizon ; and to tend the flame of national pride, which, with sincerity of purpose and fervour of soul, constitute the motive power of great enterprises. Intellectual experiments have not in our own day been unfruitful of results. Early in this century the philosopher Arago organised a literary propaganda in Paris, before which Louis Philippe in the end vanished like a spectre. Dr. Newman and a few of his friends in Oxford attacked the Puritanism of the English Church with results with which we are all familiar. One or two Westminster reviewers, and two or three Manchester manufacturers, reversed the commercial policy of England in less than a dozen years. Do not be deterred by the manifest difficulties of the task. The task is difficult but noble, for it is better to have the teaching of a people than the governing of them. Nor shall such labour lack its fitting reward, for toil and sacrifice in a generous cause are among the keenest enjoyments given to man.

IRISH LITERATURE:

Its Origin, Environment, and Influence.

BY

GEORGE SIGERSON, M.D., M.Ch., &c.,

Fellow of the Royal University of Ireland.
Corresponding Member of the Societies of Anthropology,
Clinic, and Physiological Psychology of Paris,

&c., &c.

IRISH LITERATURE: ITS ORIGIN, ENVIRONMENT, & INFLUENCE.[1]

––––◆◦◆––––

Two worlds commemorate that great adventure of Columbus, who, four centuries ago, after tragic effort, sailed forth from Huelva, and at last found the fringe of a new continent. He opened its gates to the kingdoms of Europe, but that vast region had been ages before discovered by the ships of the daring sea-kings who gave it the name of " Great Ireland "—a prophetic name.

These men we know ; Brendan and Cabot, too, we know ; but who shall tell of him who first, setting his prow against the western sunlight, drove into the dark mists of the Un-

[1] Being the substance of a Lecture delivered at the Opening of the Irish National Literary Society—in Dublin, Sir C. G. Duffy in the chair.

known, and discovered Ireland ? Forgotten
are his name and race, forgotten his struggles,
who must have been his own king, counsellor,
and guard, in an adventure greater by far, in
comparison, than that of the Genoese. But
these things we can tell of the primeval
colonists of our land. When the great
migrations of mankind streamed over Europe,
in many branching currents, those were not
the least valorous who went first and farthest.
When the Northern Ocean and the Atlantic
billows set bounds to their travel, those must
have been amongst the bravest of heart, the
most skilled of hand, and the most aspiring
of mind, who shaped, stored, equipped, and
manned the boats that were launched upon
these strange seas to confront all terrors.
And it may be a comfort to know, in view of
prevalent hypotheses, that the stock of the
Anthropoids never went through evolutions
in this country. Whatever may have happened elsewhere, the beings who first leaped
upon our shores must have been among the
foremost in the developed attributes of manhood.

These isles were to the ancients what
America has been to modern Europe, and

more. The apparent course of the sun
seemed an invitation, and ever-flying hope
showed, in the splendour of its setting, the
glories of the Hesperides. When Pytheas of
Massilia saw the Teutons in the region of the
Elbe, he rejected the view that they had
migrated, in favour of the theory that they
were autochthonoi, or products of the place,
for it was inconceivable that so dreary a
territory could attract rational beings. It was
otherwise as regards Ireland. The rumour
of its fairness seems to have reached Homer ;
to this verdant isle of Ogygia Ulysses came,
and here Calypso welcomed and wailed him.

The land must have appeared very beautiful
to those first comers who had traversed the
desolate wastes and shaggy forests of the
continent, but its aspect was not altogether
that of to-day. Green pastures there were,
where the wild deer browsed, and a wonderful
profusion of flowers, and mountain moors
that seemed mantled in purple and gold.
But there were also the mysteries of dark
forests of sombre yew, balsamic pine, and
immemorial oak, where lurked the fierce wild
bull, lean wolf, and other foes of life, now
like them extinct. We dwell above their

remains, for the Book of Nature is a palimp-
sest where the record of a new life is written
over the dead letter of the old.

Men coming to a new home bring with
them a stock of ideas, some ancestral, some
acquired on the way. They obtain others
from the suggestions of their surroundings
after arrival. In the excitement of change,
in the presence of novel phenomena and new
experience, the eye is made keen, the senses
are quickened, and the brain is stimulated to
the utmost. The rapid climatic variations of
their insular abode must have affected those
accustomed to more constant continental
atmospheres. The earliest remnants of our
literature reveal a people who were—or as, I
think, who had become in these conditions—
very sensitive to the things of nature, to
whom fair objects of heaven and earth gave
joy, and whose exalted imagination saw
mystery in new phenomena. These (common
things to us) contradicted their experience,
and the unknown causes were identified with
unseen beings. What wonder if sudden
gusts unaccountable, light twirling eddies,
mists marching through ravines and gorges,
should mask the invisible powers! Man was

face to face with nature, vibrating with every change, affected by every influence. His weapons had a secret life within, and the shield of the champion sounded when one of the Three Waves of Erin rose roaring in foam.

The aspect of the living waters was ever present, in the surging seas, the full rivers in all the plains, the liquid voice of streams in every glen, and the silent, mystical lakes among the mountains. Sometimes the waters were troubled, and they saw therein the struggles of gigantic serpents — ancestral memories of extinct animals, or reminiscences of experience in other regions. Sometimes the waters sank, or, suddenly rushing up, overwhelmed the abodes of men, owing, they fancied, to some pledge broken to the invisible deities. These strange phenomena, which have given cause for so many weird legends, I have correlated with those that precede or accompany earthquake action. It has seemed to me probable that there were, of old, beyond our western coasts, islands, which, owing to the same seismical cause, have sunk beneath the ocean level. The memory of their existence, and the fact of their absence, might well give rise to those strange and beautiful traditions of the Lands of Youth, of Life, of Virtues—their mystical appearance and disappearance—which for ages inspired the imagination of the poets. When successive waves of invaders had flowed over the land, the earliest—driven into the woods, mountains, and remote isles—assumed mythical proportions in the minds of the later comers, and, in the haze of knowledge, the land and all its far islands became peopled with a population of phantoms.

That is the cloud-background of our history, the despair of arid annalists, which contains the Nibelungen treasure of our ancient literature. We do not look there for precise date, but for the lightning-flash of ideas in the darkness of the dawn. It was the Heroic Age of Ireland, when, as in Greece and Rome, all was gigantic, Titanic, or divine. On the mountain peaks of time man saw his own image in the midst of clouds, like the spectres of the Brocken, exaggerated, majestic and terrible. In such conditions the towers of Ilion rose, Hector and Achilles fought, and Olympus helped the fray. Hence the Epic which has thrilled the world, and which, long ages later, broke the chains of the Turk, and made Greece a nation. That Epic stands alone, nor should we desire to have ideas cast in the same mould. Such desire is the defect of stereotyped thought, which does not understand that to have something diverse and original is to possess a treasure. Our ancient literature must be judged by itself, on its intrinsic merits as the articulate expression of independent humanity. If a standard is required, let it be compared with the non-classic literatures of the western world, and it will be found to rise tall and fair above them, like an Alpine peak which has caught the morning light whilst darkness reigns below.

It is certain that intellectual cultivation existed in Ireland long before the coming of St. Patrick. We have the laws at the revision of which he assisted, and I assert that, speaking biologically, such laws could not emanate from any race whose brains had not been subject to the quickening influences of education for many generations. Granting even that Christianity came before his day, there are yet abounding proofs that our ancient literature arose in pre-Christian days, so closely do its antique characters cling to it. Unquestionably no nation ever so revered its men of learning. They rewarded that reverence by giving immortal life to its heroes, and by winning for that people the respect of modern scholarship. I wish I could say of modern Ireland. But our people, generally, drink no more at the high head-fountains of their island-thought. This is one of the greatest losses which can befall a nation, for it loses thus its birthright, that central core of ideas round which new ideas would develop naturally, grow and flourish, as they never can on alien soil. There is a tone of sincerity in the ancient narratives which cannot exist in imported thought, and we are apt to lose inspiring examples of manful striving, loyal comradeship, truthful lives, chivalric courtesy, and great-minded heroism. It is true that so we escape some crude conceptions and improbable wonders. But, as in the physical order, each man seems to pass through various phases of racial development, so the individual in youth has tastes similar to those manifested by the race in its youth. Every people has at first its ideals, simple, sincere, and great, mingled with myths that stimulate the imagination. Every young generation has similar wants, and will seek to satisfy them, if not here, then elsewhere, in a literature that debases the germing ideals, dwarfs the mind, and soils the imagination.

With roots deep struck in the soil, the literature of the Irish Gael and commingled races grew vigorously from its own stock and threw out luxuriant branches and fair blooms. From the first, it exhibited characters peculiarly its own. But these were not what are considered Irish, in latter days : and here let me say that I am taken with dismay when I find some of my patriotic young friends deciding what is and what is not the Irish style in prose and the Irish note in poetry. We all know what is meant. But it is scarcely too much to say that you may search through all the Gaelic literature of the nation, and find many styles, but not this. If it ever existed, it existed outside of our classic literature, in a rustic or plebeian dialect. It must be counted, but to make it exclusive would be to impose fatal fetters on literary expression. As in other countries, there were not one but many styles, differing with the subject, the writer, and the age. At one period, we shall find works characterised by curt, clear and ringing sentences ; at another the phrase moves embarrassed by its own luxuriance.

Still more remote from the popular notion, and far more emphatic, are the characteristics of Irish Gaelic versification of which there were many kinds. I shall give a summary of the rules which govern the formation of one species only, the *Dan direach*, or Direct Metre, of which, however, there are several varieties :

1. The lines must have a certain number of syllables.

2. There must be four lines in each quatrain of two couplets. The sense may be complete in the couplet, but must be complete in the quatrain.

3. Concord must be observed ; *i.e.*, two words (not being prepositions or particles) in each line must begin with a vowel or with the same consonant. If these alliterated words be the last two, the concord is perfect, if not, it is an improper concord. The third and last lines must have perfect concord.

4. Correspondence must be observed. The bards grouped the consonants into five classes, according to the characters of the sound. Perfect correspondence demanded that the end

words in two lines should agree in possessing letters of the same class. [This may sometimes result in what we call rhyme.] If only the vowels rhyme, whilst the consonants are disregarded, then this is termed imperfect concordance.

5. Termination required the final word of each couplet to be one syllable longer than the final word in the preceding line.

6. Union is another essential. Similar to correspondence, in some respects, the same vowels need not be repeated—it suffices that they belong to the same class ; the final word of one line chimes with a central word in the next.

There are other rules besides, but these are surely enough to prove that classic Irish verse was an extremely elaborate affair. It would be impossible to adapt the English language to verse so intricate. Its existence betrayed a highly refined development of the organs of speech and of hearing, which latter is what we should expect from the musical taste and skill of the race. From such rules, we can readily understand that the bardic corporation was competent to carry this refinement of technic, and to develop an intricacy of meaning to such a degree, that the outer world required an explanation. Some of the poems of Seancan Torpeist, in the seventh century, were quite as unintelligible as the most obscure of Browning's, but, unlike Browning, he was always able to translate them to a puzzled prince. Poets seemed to have a natural tendency in the direction of over-elaboration ; they had been judges until they developed technicalities and an artificial law language, so that neither suitors nor audience could understand them. Then the princes interposed, adding laymen to the court. With their poetic tongue there was no interference, until it had been unduly exercised in oppressing the chiefs.

Now, if we examine the mechanism of any of these elaborate verses, we shall perceive that it contains a lesson greater than has been hitherto noticed. Open the Book of Kells and look at one of the initial letters, with its wonderful intricacy of interwoven lines, its exquisite grace of form, and marvellous delicacy of tint. The first glance shows it to be a beautiful work of art, and at once we recognise that it must have been produced by men whose minds, eyes, and hands had been cultivated to the highest degree. It is not the product of the training and refining of an individual or of a generation, but of a series of successive individuals in many generations. Than some of these initial letters nothing of the kind seems to have ever been made so beautiful before, nor anything since. Thus human skill in particular departments may ascend progressively till it reach its zenith and then gradually decline. Mankind acquires, but loses also ; its advance in one direction may mean retreat in another. And as works such as these are indices to the development of refinement, and to the co-operation of certain qualities and senses in man, these also must have their time of rise and fall.

Now the form-and-colour picture presented by one of these fine initials is, in another department, the sound-picture presented by Gaelic verse. A little examination shows that, besides possessing the sounds we recognise, and those which other Europeans nations have noticed, the ancient Irish composers noted, identified and employed other and more subtle shades of sound. Consider this question for a moment, for it has a physiological as well as a literary interest. We all know what the term rhyme now means in English : the sound-echo of vowels and consonants in two or more terminal words.[1] It has many charms, but tends to become monotonous in long poems ; hence authors sometimes abandon it completely for blank verse, or, using it, endeavour to evade the danger of monotony by alternating the rhyme, carrying over the sense, or varying the length of line. Now this comes of narrowing the conditions. There is no cause, save custom and imperfect audition, why only the last vowel and consonant should be echoed. The ear recognises the echo of the initial letter, or of initial consonant and vowel, in concord or alliteration. Readers of Spanish dramas and of Irish street ballads notice also the chime of the accented vowel, the vowel-rhyme, or *assonante*, although the consonants differ. But the ancient Irish, in addition to these, had also other varieties, such as the correspondence between letters of the same class. This avoided the monotony produced by a reiteration of exactly the same

---

[1] But not now of entire words, as in the *rime riche* of the French, where *livre* (book) rhymes with *livre* (pound). English "perfect" rhyme is an incomplete word-echo, which secures some variety.

letter, whilst it repeated the sound with a harmonious variation, and maintained a delicate airy phantom-chime which must have been delightful to the educated ear.

In connection with this question of sound-echo I have a proposition to put forward which may well seem startling. Of all the literary possessions of the human race, the wide world over, nothing now seems to us so constant, so universal, so eternal as rhyme. Now the fact is that rhyme was quite unknown to all the dialects of Europe, with one exception, for some centuries after the Christian era. The Greeks and the Romans wrote much poetry, but never rhymed it.[1] Their metrical system was elaborate, satisfactory, and pleasing, but it did not recognise the concordant chime of syllables. Again, there is no recognition of rhyme, as the term is now understood, in any of the Gothic dialects previous to the ninth century.

Now, what are we to infer from all this? Here I state my proposition, which is, that

[1] Sporadic exceptions of course are found in Ovid's occasional leonine lines. It is suggestive that he lived long and died amidst Scythians, from whom the Irish Gael deduce their descent.

the human ear had not then acquired the power of distinguishing and taking pleasure in these sound-echoes or repetitions which we call rhymes. That these would have been adopted, could they have been discriminated, must be inferred from their quick-extending popularity when introduced, and their subsequent universal prevalence.

Some years ago, a German professor introduced, and Mr. Gladstone, with the characteristic vigour of his many-sided mind, supported the theory that primitive man was partially colour-blind, that he could not discriminate well between differing hues. Many passages from the classic authors were adduced in support of this hypothesis, and the argument is based largely on the paucity or descriptive incompleteness of the colour-epithets. But, I venture to think that both these eminent authors would have considered their case strengthened beyond cavil had there been an entire absence of colour-epithets. That is my case : there is an entire absence of rhyme from the classic compositions and from the Gothic dialects, in the early ages, and therefore we must infer that the producers were deaf to the nice distinctions of chiming sounds. In other words, they were rhyme-deaf.'

Whence, then, came this new faculty with which mankind has been endowed? There can be no doubt that all the European races, spread as they now are over the world, are indebted for this great gift, which has quickened, delighted, elevated, and ennobled them for ages, to the Celts, and demonstrably to the ancient Irish. That seems a great claim to make—so great that when an Irishman makes it, one might suppose exaggeration ; but foreign scholarship confesses it in part, and the facts render its acceptance imperative. In our most ancient poems, such as that assigned to Lugad, son of Ith (who flourished long before the Christian era), where the language is archaic, full end-rhymes (of consonants and of vowels) are found amongst other examples of perfect correspondence.¹

Granting that the ancient Irish possessed the gift of discerning and composing rhymes before other European nations, as well as a highly developed metric machinery, another question may arise. It might be alleged that,

¹ *E.g.*, in its end-words : *tracht, eácht, fuácht, ruacht,*

confined apart in an island remote from the Continent, Irish methods could in no way affect the literature of the central and southern peoples, whilst as regards the northern, it might be urged that the Irish had no points of contact with them except where sword met sword. And for this contention, which, I shall prove erroneous, support may indeed be found in some of our chroniclers and others who seem to imagine that fighting, not thinking, is the glory of nations, and so exaggerate the first and show a practical contempt for the last.

Before entering on that topic, let me add another observation. The earlier development of auditory power in the ancient Irish, their keen discrimination of subtle sound-agreements and differences, did not stand alone. It must have been correlated with a corresponding evolution of the faculty of articulation, and, as this process went on, language as well as literature was consequently influenced. Other senses evidently shared in the development. In those initial letters, already mentioned, there is overflowing evidence of acute visual perception of colour, whilst appreciation of grace of outline and form is proved also from the writing of our oldest manuscripts, the finely wrought implements of metal, and the admirable shape of some of the flint arrow-heads, fashioned before metal was supposedly known. Mankind may lose what it has acquired (though not neces- sarily the inner aptitude), and with the ancient language is passing away some of the articula- tion-gains, as with our ancient civilisation ·have disappeared some of the educated powers of eye, and ear, and hand.

It occurs to me that from the mechanism of a people's literature, the composition of its metric especially, we can deduce conclusions as to the qualities and capacities in social and governmental matters. Building up verse may be correlated with the building up of a State, for it is an index of constructive power. The rhythmical tramp of the hexameter of Hellas and Rome, and the sustained strength of their great epics, re-appear in the disci- plined tread of phalanx and legion, and the long-continued control of their rule. In the ancient Irish metric there was less of the rhythmic tread, and probably, as a conse- quence, much less sustained power exhibited, whilst there is a great capacity for detail, a special aptitude for fine arrangements and nice distinctions. Our ancient laws and history reveal the existence of great capacity for complex social mechanism with a minor grasp of dominating and sustained control. The character of our metric might have changed had the race developed a strong central authority. In support of this speculation, I think it may be said that in France and England the classic form, borrowed from Rome, ruled with autocracy and disappeared with the theory of the right divine. The Revolution revolutionised poetry as well as politics.

It was a splendid idea of the bards to conjure back Oisin from the land of Youth, and present him and St. Patrick—types of Paganism and Christianity — in dramatic debate. The great passionate character of Oisin, his vivid love of battle and the chase, his generous spirit, his pathetic regret for lost kin and comrades, with his fiery flashes of revolt, constitute a creation in literature. No wonder that, even though amplified and altered in the garb of another language, the great conception left its impress on a later age. But I cite it here for a special reason, because it may also be taken as typifying the meeting and

interaction of ancient Irish and Roman literatures. Christianity gave the Irish that cohe-
sive organisation which their political system
lacked, and the great schools took new vigour
and vitality. Their rapid and wide-extended
reputation shows that this must have been a
pre-cultured people who could thus throw
themselves so alertly into new study and so
quickly conquer fame. The island became
the University of Europe, whither students
came from many foreign lands, and where
they were warmly welcomed, supplied with
food and books, and all gratuitously. But
never in any land had learning such an
explosive power upon a people as upon the
Irish. Elsewhere it merely gave limited impulses. Here, no sooner had scholars trained
themselves in academic studies than all the
old adventurous spirit of the nation revived,
and, ignoring minor ambitions, they swarmed
off, like bees from a full hive, carrying with
them the honey of knowledge and the ability
to create other centres that should be celebrated for all times.

They are known to have been the first
settlers in Iceland. They penetrated to
Athens, and helped potently to revive or

establish the study of Greek in Europe. Some lines of their influences only may be noticed here, but these are remarkable. St. Sedulius (Siadal), A.D. 430, introduced from the Irish the terminal sound-echo or rhyme into Latin verse. This innovation was made in hymns, and as some of these, on account of their beauty and style, were adopted and chanted in the Church (as some till this day are sung), their influence in educating the ear and popularising rhyme over Christendom was incalculable. Take this example of inter-woven echoes :

" A solis **o**rtus car*dine*, a**d**usque terræ limi*tem*,
Christum **c**anamus princi*pem*, natum Maria vir*gine*."[1]

Sedulius also produced a work of sustained power in hexameter verse, consisting of five books of nearly 1,800 lines, entitled Carmen Paschale, or The Paschal Song. It was the first great Christian Epic, and opened the way for all which came after.

[1] These rhymes are more subtly complete than may be supposed, for the chiming syllables are enriched by this, that the preceding consonants **d** and **g** (as " soft "), and **t** and **p** (as " hard "), give class-chimes. Besides this, we have alliteration of two vowels in the first line, and of two consonants in the second.

Now, in this great poem, characterised by so much originality and dramatic power, Sedulius impresses certain marked Irish peculiarities upon the classic hexameter. Thus, in the following passage, we find not only examples of " concord " in the alliterated letters, but also of " correspondence " in the terminal rhymes :

> "Neve quis ignoret, speciem crucis esse *colendam*,
> Quæ Dominum portavit ovans, ratione, p*otenti*
> Quattuor inde plagas quadrati colligit *orbis.*
> Splendidus auctoris de vertice fulget *Eous*,
> Occiduo sacræ lambuntur sidere pl*antæ* .
> Arcton dextra tenet, medium læva erigit a*xem.*"

The influence of this remarkable epic, read as it was in all the Irish (and all the Christian) schools on the Continent and in Britain, must have been immense. The systematic adoption by its author of rhyme, assonant and consonant, and of alliteration, must have moulded the forms of subsequent literary production in all the nascent languages of Europe, north and south, as it taught them the art of alliteration, of assonant, and of consonant rhymes.

The influence of St. Brendan was not less vast. If the tale of his voyage to the

West, and his arrival in a land of fair birds
and great rivers be true, he discovered America
a thousand years before Columbus. In any
case, this voyage to the Land of the Blessed
stimulated the imagination of generations.
It has been termed a prelude to the " Divina
Commedia," and, taken with other mystical
visions, which, starting from Ireland, circulated over the Continent, it doubtless helped
to direct the great genius of Dante. In a
similar manner an Irish visionary tale of St.
Patrick's Purgatory, transferred into the
Continental languages, gave origin to one
of Calderon's Spanish dramas.

This voyage of Brendan was influential in
another direction—in the discovery of America. Columbus studied the narrative. Hrafn
of Limerick, the Norse voyager, thoroughly
knew it, as did others of his nation, such as
Leif and his friends. But there is direct proof
of its coercive power. As you sail into Bristol,
you must pass under a high hill which is
known to this day as St. Brendan's Hill.[1]
There was a little chapel to St. Brendan on
its summit, because of the reverence which all
seamen, whether Norse, Saxon, or Celt, pro-

[1] Hunt, " History of Bristol, 1884."

fessed for the sailor-saint. Now, in 1480 two British merchants equipped two ships to sail to the Isle of Brasylle in the west of Ireland, but after nine weeks' vain voyaging they put into an Irish port. The Bristol men (who were largely of Norse blood) were not discouraged. In 1498, the Spaniard De Ayala informed his sovereign that for seven years they had every year sent out two, three, or four light ships in search of the Island of Brazil (*i.e.*, the Irish " Hy-Breasail ") and the Seven Cities. The adventure was under the direction of Cabot, the Genoese, who discovered the northern shore of America a year before Columbus reached its more inviting isles. Thus, either St. Brendan's voyage is a fact, and then he was the true First Discoverer ; or it is a fiction, and then it was the direct cause of that discovery. This were a remarkable result of the power of the imaginative literature of the ancient Irish. No other people on earth can claim the discovery of a Continent as the result of a romance.

Whilst some of the early Christians deprecated the study of the pagan classics, the Irish held large and more liberal views. This was peculiarly true of St. Columbanus. Authoritative, inflexible, a daring missionary, his royal mind embraced the wide domain of letters. His eloquence is confessed. His monastic maxims are described as fit for a brotherhood of philosophers, whilst his wit is shown in his lighter poems, his culture in the adoption of old Greek metre, and his Irish training in the terminal rhymes in the alliteration of many of his verses. The following show both final rhymes and concordant initials :

> " Dilexerunt tenebras tetras magis quam *lucem*,
> Imitari contemnunt vitæ **D**ominum d*ucem:*
> **V**elut in somnis **r**egnent una hora læta*ntur*,
> Sed æterna tormenta adhuc illius para*ntur*." [1]

His national characteristics were impressed on the great School of Bobbio, which he created, in which he died, and whence his influence long radiated over Italy and the North.

Entering the old Cathedral of Aachen, or

[1] In the third line, the letters **v** and **r** are in (imperfect) concord. They belong to the same class of "light" consonants, from which it might be inferred that the ancient Irish did not roll the letter *r*.

Aix-la-Chapelle, you will be shown the great
marble chair in which, cold as the marble,
Charlemagne sat enthroned, sceptre in hand,
robed in imperial purple, and with diadem
on brow, dead. So he sate when, a century
and a half later, Otho and his riotous
courtiers broke open the vault and stood
sobered and appalled before the majesty of
death. On that same chair he sate, in similar
apparel, but with the light of life in his eyes,
the new Augustus of a new Empire, when
two Irish wanderers were brought before him.
In the streets of the city in which he hoped
to revive the glory of Athens and the great-
ness of Rome, they had been heard to cry
out : "Whoso wants wisdom, let him come
to us and receive it, for we have it for sale."
Their terms were not onerous—food and
raiment. Their claims stood the test. One,
Albinus, was sped to Pavia in Italy ; the
other, Clement, had the high honour of
superseding the learned Anglo-Saxon Alcuin
in the Palatine school of the Imperial city.
Here, he taught the *trivium* and *quadrivium*
—grammar, rhetoric, dialectic, and arith-
metic, music, geometry, and astronomy—the
seven arts. In his school sate Charlemagne

under the school-name of David, the members of his family each under an academic name, and with these the members of the cortége, the Palatins or Paladins, destined to power and feats of fame. The teaching of the Irish professors here must have had considerable influence on the literature (*e.g.*, the *Chansons de Geste*) which afterwards took its heroes from their scholars. Their authority was enhanced by the fact that Charlemagne himself worked with his Irish professors at a revision of the Gospels on the Greek and on the Syriac text.[1]

In the crash and chaos which followed soon after his death, when feudal vassals, strong as their nominal suzerain, lived an isolated warlike life and forgot letters, in the confusion caused by the shifting about of nations from the east and north—partly a rebound from imperial coercion—certain Irish names shine with especial splendour. The first is that of Johannes Scotus Erigena. Of unquestioned learning, versed in Greek, he was the founder of Scholastic Philosophy. This affects us still, for in Scholasticism, as in a forge, the intellect of the Middle Ages was fired, tempered, and

[1] Thegan ; Pithou : Opp. cvii.

made supple, keen, and trenchant. Hence, with all its powers awakened and under alert control, it was rendered fit for the production of the new sciences of modern times. Nor should it be forgotten that Fearghal the Geometer had but recently died, whose daring scientific speculations as to the Antipodes had shocked the stiff-minded Saxon Boniface. Dicuil brought exact science to bear on a cognate subject, in his work on the measurement of the earth —a work which has been republished in several foreign countries, but never in his native land.

The multitudes of students who flocked to Paris to hear Erigena, contented with couches of straw in the Rue de la Fouarre and old halls of the University, were not the last who invaded it to hear an eloquent Irishman. Four hundred years later, in the very beginning of the fourteenth century, another, and perhaps a still more illustrious, representative of Irish thought, in the person of Duns Scotus the Subtle Doctor, throned it over the minds of men. So great was his renown that when in 1308 he came to Cologne the city accorded him a triumphal entry, more splendid than a king's.

Far, in every sense, from such ovations is

that desolate island off the Scotch coast, where, in the sixth century, "a grey eye turned ever in vain" towards that Ireland "where the songs of the birds are so sweet, where the clerks sing like birds, where the young are so gentle, the old so wise, and the maidens so fair to wed." The exile charges his parting pupil to bear his blessing, part to Alba, part to Ireland—"seven times may she be blessed. . . . My heart is broken in my breast. If death comes to me suddenly, it will be because of the great love I bear the Gael."

Columba is the first Irish poet of exile—of which our nation has such sad experience since. His poetry, like his life, is instinct with the deepest affection for his native land, whilst his work has been the most fruitful in influence over the intellectual development of Scotland and England. From the island of Iona, chiefly, went forth that persuasive power which carried education over Britain. The majority of the Anglo-Saxon kingdoms, all the North of England, where English learning and literature took its rise, were bathed in an Irish intellectual atmosphere. Caedmon began his song in this environment, and when

later, in the eight century, English Aldhelm
first wrote rhymed Latin verse, it was because
he had been a pupil of the Irishman Mailduff,
the first Abbot of Malmesbury.[1]

To speak of literary relations between the
Irish and the Norse may provoke some
derision. Were not these the fierce sea-kings
the "Danes," whose delight was in war, and
whose avocation in peace was the plunder
of shrines ? They were, however, paradoxical
enough to build Christ Church, and to richly
endow it. And it is also a curious fact that,
previous to three great invasions of other
countries, for which they are severely blamed,
they had been appealingly besought for help
by their supposed victims. Iarl Hacon went
to oppose the aggressions of the Emperor
Otho ; King Harald Sigurdson to avenge
wrongs inflicted by English Harold ; and
Iarl Sigurd of the Orkneys (whose mother
was an Irishwoman) could not resist the
appeal of Irish beauty in distress—in the
person of Queen Brian Borumha, who was
mother of the Norse king of Dublin.

There were, in fact, many and important
matrimonial alliances between the Irish and

[1] Malmesbury is a modification of Mailduff's burg.

Norse princes, who often joined forces against
foes. This happened at Clontarf, where the
Irish of Leinster had the alliance of the Dublin
and Orkney Norse, whilst Brian brought up
the Danes of Limerick. This battle, let me
remark, is described in the literature of both
countries, and in both descriptions there are
omens and spiritual beings such as signalise
the epic of Homer. So great was Norse influence over Ireland that three of our provinces
retain the Northern name-endings, and many
a headland and bay has a Norse appellation.
They delighted in the loveliness of the land.
Linnæus, in latter days, fell on his knees
before the splendour of a furze-bush in blossom,
and we can readily imagine how tears came
into the eyes of the Arctic rovers when they
beheld the fresh green of Ovoca or were
dazzled by the crimson and gold of Benn
Edair, which they called Howth.[1] Irish
music charmed them, and even now some of
our old airs awake echoes along the norland
fiords.[2]

The latest and most distinguished authori-

[1] *I.e.*, Hoved, The Head.
[2] Hr. Sjöden, the eminent Swedish harper, noted several Scandinavian airs but slightly varied from the Irish.

ties [1] declare that Irish literature has largely influenced that of the Scandinavians. Their Heroic Age was much later than ours, from the end of the ninth to the eleventh centuries, when the ambition of Harold Haarfagre to imitate the imperial methods of Charlemagne had driven the independent princes to far isles or foreign voyages. They were in close and continuous contact in peace and war with the Irish, " whose ancient civilisation was superior and therefore stronger." Bergen, the old Norse capital, possessed a church dedicated to St. Columba, and the revered relics of its patron, St. Sunniva, an Irish maiden! As you sail into Rejkiavik, the capital of Iceland, you pass the Westman Isles, so-called because of the Irish who had visited and dwelt there. Now Iceland—that strange attractive island, where cold white snow covers the hot volcanic heart —is the old home of the Sagas. It had been first peopled by some Irish monks. Another settlement took place when Queen Aud— widow of White Olaf, the Norse King of Dublin—went thither on the death of her son. Norsemen and Irishmen, her kinsfolk and de-

---

[1] Messrs. Vigfusson and York Powell in " Corpus Poeticum Boreale," &c.

pendents, accompanied her. Mr. Vigfusson, himself an Icelander, writes with a generous fairness, characteristic of the race, as follows :

" The bulk of the settlers were men who, at least for one generation, had dwelt among a Keltic population and undergone an influence which an old and strongly marked civilisation invariably exercises among those brought under it—an attraction which in this particular case was of so potent a kind that centuries later it metamorphosed the Norman knights of the foremost European kingdom with startling rapidity into Irish chieftains." "Moreover," he adds, " we find among the emigrants of all ranks men and women of pure Irish and Scottish blood, as also as many sprung from mixed marriages, and traces of this crossing survive in the Irish names borne by some of the foremost characters of the Heroic Age of Iceland, especially the poets, of whom it is also recorded that they were dark men." He considers that this close intercourse with the Celts had to do with heightening and colouring the strong but somewhat prosaic Teuton imagination into that finer and more artistic spirit manifested in the Icelandic Saga. The classic land of the Saga was in West Iceland,

and there also the proportion of Irish blood was greatest. On the Norsemen who still remain there the Irish influence was yet more effective and powerful. Mr. Vigfusson makes an observation, which is a touching and keen reproach to those on whom it devolves to publish the manuscript materials of ancient Irish literature. He writes : " Only when it is possible to judge fairly of the remains of the Keltic literature of the ninth, tenth, and eleventh centuries, can any definite conception of the influence it exerted on Icelandic, Norse, and English literature be properly estimated." [1]

With the great Sagas, the fame of which has spread abroad as their strong dramatic character deserves, Northern literature possesses the no less celebrated Eddas. These Eddic poems "discover an ideal of beauty," writes Mr. York Powell, "an aerial unearthly fairy world, and a love of nature which we do not find in the Saga." They also reveal that those who composed them were familiar with more southern scenes and manners ; and the poems are shown to be the mental offspring of the men " who won Waterford and Limerick and kinged it in York and East England."

[1] Vigfusson, Prolegomena to Sturlunga Saga.

" It is well to remark," he adds, "that among
the first poets we have any knowledge of, the
majority are of mixed blood with an Irish
ancestress not far back in the family tree. . . .
Their physical characteristics, dark hair and
black eyes, like Sighvat and Kormack,[1] their
reckless passion and wonderful fluency are
also non-Teutonic and speak of their alien
descent." In Bragi's Eddic poem there is a
very manifest introduction of a characteristic
Irish rhyme-method.

Thus we have it on unquestionable authority
that the noble Norse literature, which occupies
a position of the greatest importance, dominating as it does the Teutonic world, was itself
the offspring, in a certain sense, of our ancient
Irish literature. Irish literary training and
talent presided over and took part in its composition, gave dramatic vividness to its narrative—grace, method, and myths to its poetry.

With this knowledge in mind you will look
with better insight into the story of the Norsemen in Ireland, and see them, no longer as a
cloud of barbarians, but as brave adventurous
knights whose voyages fringed our seas with a
murmur of song, and whose cities, in quiet

[1] From the Irish name, Cormac.

times, were the favourite resort of Irishmen skilled in letters and all the arts of peace and war. "Why should we think of faring home?" sang King Magnus. "My heart is in Dublin. I shall not return in autumn to the ladies of Nidaros. Youth makes me love the Irish girl better than myself."

Considering how often and how constantly the prejudice of the ignorant prevents a good understanding between neighbours, whether these be individuals or nations, I have sometimes thought of writing a book to be entitled: "The Good Deeds of our Enemies." Too often do we find writers stopping at nothing to cover the foe with obloquy. By this they put out their own eyes and blind our moral sight. Proceeding on a different principle, I should show enemies, not in their conflicts, but in their concessions, and the picture would give a truer idea of mankind, for it is surprising how many kind offices were mutually interchanged between foemen—even in this very country—who are always represented as savage, ruthless, and exterminating.

Ireland has been able to act upon the literature of the Continent and of Britain in three ways: first, directly, next by means of its pupils on the Continent, and finally by means of the Norse literature. The latter affected both Britain and Germany, so that the Irish spirit has had a double influence, be it much or little, upon both. Professor Morley, indeed, admits that "the story of our literature begins with the Gael"; and pointing out the intermixture of blood, he adds: "But for early frequent and various contact with the race which in its half barbarous days invented Oisin's dialogues with St. Patrick, and that quickened afterwards the Northmen's blood in France and Germany, England would not have produced a Shakespeare."

Certain it is, I think, that but for the influence of Irish literature, Shakespeare would not have produced a "Midsummer Night's Dream," "The Tempest," and "Macbeth." The aerial beings which characterise the first two plays are like those delightful melodies which Boïeldieu in "La Dame Blanche," and Flotow in "Marthe" made popular over the Continent, and which the Irish ear, suddenly attentive, recognises as Irish in spite of their foreign surroundings.[1]

[1] Shakespeare mentions an old Irish air, *Cailin og astor* (in "Henry II.", act iv., sc. 4); the air itself is give in

Teutonic poetry, in certain particulars, appears to have germinated from the seed which fell from the ripe Irish harvest. The alliteration found in " Beowulf," the first Anglo-Saxon epic, A.D. 750 (three centuries after Sedulius), seems a rather crude imitation. Rhyme was introduced into High German a century later, and this was achieved by Otfried, who had acquired the gift in that great monastry of St. Gall to which the illustrious Irish-

Queen Elizabeth's Virginal Book, so that Irish music must have been admired at her court. It is curious to see the Irish alliteration still influential in the verses attributed to her :

"The doubt of future foes exiles my present joy,
   And wit me warns to shun such snares as threaten mine
     annoy ;
   For falsehood now doth flow and subject faith doth ebb,
   Which would not be if reason ruled or wisdom weaved
     the web."

It is most interesting to observe that Shakespeare himself employs alliteration in his epitaph, and used it in a manner so closely conforming to the regular Irish system, as to suggest his acquaintance with it, e.g. :

"Good friend for Jesus' sake forbeare,
   To dig the dust enclosed here,
   Blesst be he who spares these stones,
   And cursed be he who moves my bones."

man bequeathed his·name, his spirit, and his scholarship, which long guided his many disciples.

The Nibelungen Lied and the Lay of Gudrun have been called the Iliad and the Odyssey of Germany. Both, however, have Norse originals. Now, with respect to the latter it is a remarkable but surely not a surprising thing, after all we know, that the opening scenes of the lay should be placed in Ireland. The fierce King of Ireland, Hagen (? Hacon), had a fair daughter Hilda, and to woo her for their King, Hettel of Denmark, came a number of daring champions, disguised as merchants. The wooing with music, which captures the Irish maiden's heart, the flight, pursuit, marriage and reconcilement, are told with animation. Gudrun, the daughter of Hettel's Irish wife, is the second heroine of the tale. In the Arthurian Romance of Tristan and Isolde (as in some others) there are Irish scenes and Irish characters. Isolde herself has bequeathed Dublin her name in Isolde's Tower and Chapel-isod. I need but remind you that the Arthurian Romances gave origin to Tennyson's "Idylls of the King."

The kindred peoples of France and of Spain

were naturally not less influenced than the
Teutonic races. The Romans did not give
them rhyme ; their own literature had perished ;
consequently they borrowed from the islands
to which, in Cæsar's time, the continental
Druids were sent for training. Assonant
rhyme, found in some Anglo-Norman poems,
was common in the Romance of Oc and all
related dialects. " It is clearly the Irish *Com-
harda*" (correspondence), writes an English
authority, Mr. Guest, " though not submitted
in the Romance dialects to the nice rules
which regulate its assonances in the Gaelic."

Irish literature has received gifts in return :
in the old Anglo-Saxon Mystery Play, found
in the Record Office, in the Anglo-Norman
Rhyme of Ross, in the Song of Dermott, and in
others unfortunately still unpublished. Michael
of Kildare is supposed to be our first poet in
English, and he is the pioneer-poet of satire
in that language.

This postern, which he opened into what has
since become the vast empire of literature in
English, gave entrance to many. Spenser
came to us, through it, and, caught by the
glamour of the Gael, gave us the " Faërie
Queene," wherein he immortalises some of our

scenery and pays tribute to the ancient renown of our nation :

> " Whilome when Ireland flourished in fame
> Of wealth and goodness far above the rest
> Of all that bear the British Islands name."

It is noteworthy that the great poem, which marked the revival of English letters after Chaucer, was composed in Ireland. Granting that Spenser found models in Ariosto and Tasso, yet, if he had remained in London, he might never have risen above the standard of the Palace-poets. Shakespeare in London was saved by the drama demanding an environment of popular life. Probably nothing saved Spenser but his immersion in Irish nature, which his verse so faithfully reflects. Not only are the material beauties of our country — mountains, woods, and rivers— mirrored there, but its spiritual world also. The very name of Una is Irish, and our Puca appears in trimmed English as " the Pouke," whom Shakespeare again introduces as Puck, just as our Gaelic Madb becomes " Queen Mab."

But it may be said that Spenser was ignorant of the literature of the hostile Irish nation, and so could not be influenced by it. The case is otherwise. When Eudoxus asks : " Have they any art in their compositions, or bee they anything wittie in or well savoured as poems should be ? " Spenser (as Irenæus) answers : " Yes, truely, I have caused divers of them to be translated unto me, that I might understand them, and surely they savoured of sweet wit and good invention, but skilled not of the goodly ornaments of poetry" (rather these were lost in a prose translation) ; " they were sprinkled with some pretty flowers of their naturall device, which gave good grace and comelinesse unto them."

It is a strange thing to say that Edmund Spenser, who so deprecates their "rebellious" love of liberty, might well have envied the position and influence of the Irish poets. At the Queen's Court in England he had learned "what hell it is in suing long to bide," to "eat the heart in despair," and all the miseries of dilatory patronage :

> " To fawn, to crouch, to wait, to ride, to run,
> To spend, to give, to want, to be undone."

In Ireland he saw a different state of things.

The poets might almost be described as the patrons, for theirs it was to distribute praise or dispraise in poems, "the which," says Spenser, "are held in so high regard and estimation amongst them that none dare displease them, for feare to runne into reproach through their offence, and be made infamous in the mouths of all men."

Their compositions were sung at all feasts and meetings by other persons, and these also, to his surprise, " receive great rewards and reputation." Certain it is, though strange, that Edmund Spenser, had he been least bard in the pettiest principality of Ireland, instead of being the first poet of the monarch of Great Britain, would not have died of hunger. Neglected and starving in Westminster, may he not have regretted his political efforts to destroy the one national organism which above all others had ever generously encouraged the representatives of literature ? [1]

It is a study full of interest to watch the development of the culture of the Anglo-Irish

---

[1] It has been computed that, in the petty princedom of Tyrconnell (now Donegall county nearly) the real estate allocated to maintenance of the *literati* amounted in value to £2,000 yearly, present currency.

Pale, and the continuance of that of the Irish nation. In Latin, their men of learning had long a common language, but the vernacular was not neglected. In 1600 the literary organisation was still strong, and its strength was shown in the great Bardic Contention. Thirty-two years later an assemblage of historians, antiquaries, and monks was held to collect and collate materials for the great Annals of the Kingdom. Four years the Four Masters laboured at the work, safe by the far shore of Donegall, and fortunate it was, for soon after there was no safety in the "Athens of the West"—the "University of Europe"—for those of its faithful offspring who loved learning and letters. Teacher and pupil were banned. In the midst of morasses, forests, or mountain-glens, they still studied, their bards still sang, and their minstrels played, often with outposted sentinels on the watch.

What wonder if sadness shadowed the land? But disaster may have some compensating gifts to noble natures. The true laurel when crushed yields all its inner fragrance. Deprived of their princes and deposed from their estate, the bards ceased to be learned in the classic forms of literary technic ; but they became poets of the people. The sincere voice of their hearts spoke in their song, which is brimful of passionate feeling and glowing with fair ideals. If in other times they had too often confined their efforts to the eulogy of particular princes, now it was otherwise. At the hearths of the people they sang the songs of a Nation.

Perhaps now the first idea of modern nation-hood was conceived. Now, at all events, pathos became a character of Irish literature, distinguishing it deeply from that counterfeit of late grotesque, the authors of which resemble those mutilators of men who carved the mockery of laughter upon the face of grief.

What a subject for a painter would be that meeting between the blind and hoary bard Carolan, and the young, bright-eyed child Oliver Goldsmith ! The venerable aspect of the ancient Celtic poet he never forgot. " His songs," he says, " in general may be compared to those of Pindar ; they have frequently the same flight of imagination." He had composed a concerto " with such spirit and elegance that it may be compared (for we have it still) with the finest compositions of Italy." This reminds us of the time when an enemy, Giraldus Cambrensis, declared that the skill of the Irish in music " was incomparably superior to that of any other nation."

The meeting of Carolan and Goldsmith may fitly typify the meeting of the literatures of the old nation and of the Pale—one venerable by age and glorified by genius, the other young, buoyant, and destined, like it, to be the guardian and the honour of our common country.

Irish literature is of many blends, not the product of one race but of several. It resembles the great oriel of some ancient cathedral, an illumination of many beautiful colours, some of which can never be reproduced, for the art is lost. We possess an unique treasure in that ancient literature which grew up from a cultured people, self-centred, independent of Roman discipline. Were it not for this we should look at the Northern world through Southern eyes, and, taking our view-point from the Capitol, see nothing beyond the light of the empire, but wild woods and wastes made horrid by Cimmerian darkness, and shifting hordes of quarrelsome barbarians. Yet these were the ancestors of most of the modern European peoples, and those who so depicted them were their coercive and uncomprehending foes. Our deliverance from this thraldom of an enemy's judgment abides. in the monuments of the ancient Irish.

The magic password of the Arabian bade the rugged mountain open, and admitted him to the midst of glittering jewels. The knowledge of our old literature takes us into the heart of the Cimmerian darkness, and shows it full of glowing light, it takes us into the homes and minds of one of those great nations uncomprehended of the Romans, and through that one, enables us to see the great, passionate, pathetic, wild, and generous humanity of all.

Thus our ancient literature would be invaluable if for this reason alone, that it gives a new view-point and a new vista. Its importance is augmented in this, that its reckless sincerity stands the enduring evidence of a long-vanished stage of social and intellectual development, where the fiercer and finer powers, the softer and sterner emotions of an early mankind strive and commingle with dramatic effect. If such a deposit were not extant, European scholars might well desire to go as pilgrims, like the bereaved bards, to the grave of Fergus, son of Roi, with power to call him again on earth, that he might recite the famous Táin—the lost Epic of a lost World.

It is strange that words, which are such little things—a mere breath trembling for a moment in the air — should survive the mightiest monarch and outlast the lives of empires. The generations who uttered them are silent ; the earth has grown over their homesteads, and forests have decayed above their cities. Yet out of the Dead Past speaks still the Living Voice. So, to-day, we may be illumined by the light of a star which perished a thousand years ago.

It has been said that the history of Ireland is dismal, a chronicle of defeats. But that is because writers generally make history a mere record of wars. The shadow of the swordsman obscures all else. The militant monarch or minister is always put in the foremost place and the highest position. The pigmy on a platform looks greater than the giant in his study—but only in the eyes of pigmies.

Alexander's Empire died with him, and his satraps shared the spoil. Aristotle's sceptre is over us still.

' There is a blindness which is worse than colour-blindness in the eyes which see physical, but which cannot perceive intellectual forces and effects : they will record that Roman power conquered Greece, but fail to recognise that Greek intellect conquered the conqueror. Our nation has had its changes of fortune. It has invaded others, and been itself invaded often—part of the penalty it paid for occupying the fairest isle of the old world, a penalty we might still pay had not a new world opened wide its golden gates in the West. But our defeats have not been always disasters. What seemed to have no other end than the plunder of our wealth has resulted in the enrichment of our literature, the dissemination of our ideas, and the capture of the imagination of other nations. The code, which was devised to accomplish what the most ruthless savage never designed —the annihilation of the intellect of a most intelligent nation—studded the Continent with that nation's colleges and gave to its members the glory of being illustrious leaders of men in the greatest kingdoms of the world.

Last came the great dispersal, when the descendants of those who had taught Europe for three centuries, and generously welcomed all scholars—now made ignorant by law—were driven from their hospitable land by famine. They went forth, as it is said, hewers of wood and drawers of water. In other times and places it had meant extinction as slaves under feudal rule. But mark this!—they entered into the great family of a new people, whose fundamental principle of Democracy made them equal, and whose generous nature made them welcome. They have thus been brought to the very well-spring of the new forces which have been re-shaping human society and preparing the transformation of the world. In this incomparable enterprise they are themselves a foremost force, taking part in the intellectual work with the revived vitality of a race which has found its Land of Youth.

If we had a past of shame—were we members of a nation that had never risen or had deeply fallen—these should be incentives to brave hearts to achieve work for the credit of their race. It is otherwise with us, and we dare not stand still. The past would be

our reproach, the future our disgrace. Not
foreign force, but native sloth can do us dis-
honour. If our nation is to live, it must live
by the energy of intellect, and be prepared to
take its place in competition with all other
peoples. Therefore must we work, with
earnest hearts and high ideals for the sake
of our own repute, for the benefit of mankind,
in vindication of this old land which genius
has made luminous. And remember that
whilst wealth of thought is a country's treasure, literature is its articulate voice, by which
it commands the reverence or calls for the
contempt of the living and of the coming
Nations of the Earth.

THE NECESSITY FOR DE-ANGLICISING IRELAND.

BY

DOUGLAS HYDE, LL.D.

THE NECESSITY FOR DE-ANGLICI-
SING IRELAND.[1]

WHEN we speak of "The Necessity for De-
Anglicising the Irish Nation," we mean it,
not as a protest against imitating what is
best in the English people, for that would
be absurd, but rather to show the folly of
neglecting what is Irish, and hastening to
adopt, pell-mell, and indiscriminately, everything that is English, simply because it *is*
English.

This is a question which most Irishmen
will naturally look at from a National point
of view, but it is one which ought also to
claim the sympathies of every intelligent

[1] Delivered before the Irish National Literary Society
in Dublin, November 25th, 1892.

Unionist, and which, as I know, does claim the sympathy of many.

If we take a bird's-eye view of our island to-day, and compare it with what it used to be, we must be struck by the extraordinary fact that the nation which was once, as every one admits, one of the most classically learned and cultured nations in Europe, is now one of the least so ; how one of the most reading and literary peoples has become one of the *least* studious and most *un*-literary, and how the present art products of one of the quickest, most sensitive, and most artistic races on earth are now only distinguished for their hideousness.

I shall endeavour to show that this failure of the Irish people in recent times has been largely brought about by the race diverging during this century from the right path, and ceasing to be Irish without becoming English. I shall attempt to show that with the bulk of the people this change took place quite recently, much more recently than most people imagine, and is, in fact, still going on. I should also like to call attention to the illogical position of men who drop their own language to speak English, of men who translate their euphonious Irish names into English monosyllables, of men who read English books, and know nothing about Gaelic literature, nevertheless protesting as a matter of sentiment that they hate the country which at every hand's turn they rush to imitate.

I wish to show you that in Anglicising ourselves wholesale we have thrown away with a light heart the best claim which we have upon the world's recognition of us as a separate nationality. What did Mazzini say? What is Goldwin Smith never tired of declaiming? What do the *Spectator* and *Saturday Review* harp on? That we ought to be content as an integral part of the United Kingdom because we have lost the notes of nationality, our language and customs.

It has always been very curious to me how Irish sentiment sticks in this half-way house —how it continues to apparently hate the English, and at the same time continues to imitate them; how it continues to clamour for recognition as a distinct nationality, and at the same time throws away with both hands what would make it so. If Irishmen only went a little farther they would become good English-

men in sentiment also. But—illogical as it
appears—there seems not the slightest sign or
probability of their taking that step. It is the
curious certainty that come what may Irishmen will continue to resist English rule, even
though it should be for their good, which
prevents many of our nation from becoming
Unionists upon the spot. It is a fact, and we
must face it as a fact, that although they adopt
English habits and copy England in every
way, the great bulk of Irishmen and Irish-
women over the whole world are known to
be filled with a dull, ever-abiding animosity
against her, and—right or wrong—to grieve
when she prospers, and joy when she is
hurt. Such movements as Young Irelandism,
Fenianism, Land Leagueism, and Parliamen-
tary obstruction seem always to gain their
sympathy and support. It is just because
there appears no earthly chance of their becoming good members of the Empire that
I urge that they should not remain in the
anomalous position they are in, but since
they absolutely refuse to become the one
thing, that they become the other; cultivate
what they have rejected, and build up an
Irish nation on Irish lines.

But you ask, why should we wish to make Ireland more Celtic than it is—why should we de-Anglicise it at all ?

I answer because the Irish race is at present in a most anomalous position, imitating England and yet apparently hating it. How can it produce anything good in literature, art, or institutions as long as it is actuated by motives so contradictory ? Besides, I believe it is our Gaelic past which, though the Irish race does not recognise it just at present, is really at the bottom of the Irish heart, and prevents us becoming citizens of the Empire, as, I think, can be easily proved.

To say that Ireland has not prospered under English rule is simply a truism ; all the world admits it, England does not deny it. But the English retort is ready. You have not prospered, they say, because you would not settle down contentedly, like the Scotch, and form part of the Empire. "Twenty years of good, resolute, grand-fatherly government," said a well-known Englishman, will solve the Irish question. He possibly made the period too short, but let us suppose this. Let us suppose for a moment — which is impossible — that there

were to arise a series of Cromwells in England for the space of one hundred years, able
administrators of the Empire, careful rulers of
Ireland, developing to the utmost our national
resources, whilst they unremittingly stamped
out every spark of national feeling, making
Ireland a land of wealth and factories, whilst
they extinguished every thought and every
idea that was Irish, and left us, at last, after
a hundred years of good government, fat,
wealthy, and populous, but with all our
characteristics gone, with every external that
at present differentiates us from the English
lost or dropped ; all our Irish names of
places and people turned into English names ;
the Irish language completely extinct ; the
O's and the Macs dropped ; our Irish intona-
tion changed, as far as possible by English
schoolmasters into something English ; our
history no longer remembered or taught ;
the names of our rebels and martyrs blotted
out ; our battlefields and traditions forgotten ;
the fact that we were not of Saxon origin
dropped out of sight and memory, and let me
now put the question—How many Irishmen
are there who would purchase material
prosperity at such a price ? It is exactly

such a question as this and the answer to it that shows the difference between the English and Irish race. Nine Englishmen out of ten would jump to make the exchange, and I as firmly believe that nine Irishmen out of ten would indignantly refuse it.

And yet this awful idea of complete Anglicisation, which I have here put before you in all its crudity, is, and has been, making silent inroads upon us for nearly a century.

Its inroads have been silent, because, had the Gaelic race perceived what was being done, or had they been once warned of what was taking place in their own midst, they would, I think, never have allowed it. When the picture of complete Anglicisation is drawn for them in all its nakedness Irish sentimentality becomes suddenly a power and refuses to surrender its birthright.

What lies at the back of the sentiments of nationality with which the Irish millions seem so strongly leavened, what can prompt them to applaud such sentiments as :

"They say the British empire owes much to Irish hands,
That Irish valour fixed her flag o'er many conquered lands;

And ask if Erin takes no pride in these her gallant
    sons,
Her Wolseleys and her Lawrences, her Wolfes and
    Wellingtons.

Ah ! these were of the Empire—we yield them to her
    fame,
And ne'er in Erin's orisons are heard their alien name ;
But those for whom her heart beats high and benedic-
    tions swell,
They died upon the scaffold and they pined within the
    cell."

Of course it is a very composite feeling
which prompts them ; but I believe that
what is largely behind it is the half unconscious feeling that the race which at
one time held possession of more than half
Europe, which established itself in Greece,
and burned infant Rome, is now—almost
extirpated and absorbed elsewhere—making
its last stand for independence in this island
of Ireland ; and do what they may the race of
to-day cannot wholly divest itself from the
mantle of its own past. Through early Irish
literature, for instance, can we best form some
conception of what that race really was,
which, after overthrowing and trampling on
the primitive peoples of half Europe, was

itself forced in turn to yield its speech, manners, and independence to the victorious eagles of Rome. We alone of the nations of Western Europe escaped the claws of those birds of prey ; we alone developed ourselves naturally upon our own lines outside of and free from all Roman influence ; we alone were thus able to produce an early art and literature, *our* antiquities can best throw light upon the pre-Romanised inhabitants of half Europe, and—we are our father's sons.

There is really no exaggeration in all this, although Irishmen are sometimes prone to overstating as well as to forgetting. Westwood himself declares that, were it not for Irishmen, these islands would possess no primitive works of art worth the mentioning ; Jubainville asserts that early Irish literature is that which best throws light upon the manners and customs of his own ancestors the Gauls ; and Zimmer, who has done so much for Celtic philology, has declared that only a spurious criticism can make an attempt to doubt about the historical character of the chief persons of our two epic cycles, that of Cuchullain and of Finn. It is useless elaborating this point ; and Dr. Sigerson has

already shown in his opening lecture the debt
of gratitude which in many respects Europe
owes to ancient Ireland. The dim consciousness of this is one of those things which are
at the back of Irish national sentiment, and
our business, whether we be Unionists or
Nationalists, should be to make this dim
consciousness an active and potent feeling,
and thus increase our sense of self-respect and
of honour.

What we must endeavour to never forget
is this, that the Ireland of to-day is the
descendant of the Ireland of the seventh
century, then the school of Europe and the
torch of learning. It is true that Northmen
made some minor settlements in it in the
ninth and tenth centuries, it is true that the
Normans made extensive settlements during
the succeeding centuries, but none of those
broke the continuity of the social life of the
island. Dane and Norman drawn to the
kindly Irish breast issued forth in a generation or two fully Irishised, and more Hibernian
than the Hibernians themselves, and even
after the Cromwellian plantation the children
of numbers of the English soldiers who settled
in the south and midlands, were, after forty

years' residence, and after marrying Irish wives, turned into good Irishmen, and unable to speak a word of English, while several Gaelic poets of the last century have, like Father English, the most unmistakably English names. In two points only was the continuity of the Irishism of Ireland damaged. First, in the north-east of Ulster, where the Gaelic race was expelled and the land planted with aliens, whom our dear mother Erin, assimilative as she is, has hitherto found it difficult to absorb, and in the ownership of the land, eight-ninths of which belongs to people many of whom always lived, or live, abroad, and not half of whom Ireland can be said to have assimilated.

During all this time the continuation of Erin's national life centred, according to our way of looking at it, not so much in the Cromwellian or Williamite landholders who sat in College Green, and governed the country, as in the mass of the people whom Dean Swift considered might be entirely neglected, and looked upon as hewers of wood and drawers of water ; the men who, nevertheless, constituted the real working population, and who were living on in the hopes of better days ; the men who have since made America, and have within the last ten years proved what an important factor they may be in wrecking or in building the British Empire. These are the men of whom our merchants, artisans, and farmers mostly consist, and in whose hands is to-day the making or marring of an Irish nation. But, alas, *quantum mutatus ab illo!* What the battleaxe of the Dane, the sword of the Norman, the wile of the Saxon were unable to perform, we have accomplished ourselves. We have at last broken the continuity of Irish life, and just at the moment when the Celtic race is presumably about to largely recover possession of its own country, it finds itself deprived and stript of its Celtic characteristics, cut off from the past, yet scarcely in touch with the present. It has lost since the beginning of this century almost all that connected it with the era of Cuchullain and of Ossian, that connected it with the Christianisers of Europe, that connected it with Brian Boru and the heroes of Clontarf, with the O'Neills and O'Donnells, with Rory O'More, with the Wild Geese, and even to some extent with the men of '98. It has lost all that they had—language, traditions, music, genius, and ideas. Just when we should be starting to build up anew the Irish race and the Gaelic nation—as within our own recollection Greece has been built up anew— we find ourselves despoiled of the bricks of nationality. The old bricks that lasted eighteen hundred years are destroyed ; we must now set to, to bake new ones, if we can, on other ground and of other clay. Imagine for a moment the restoration of a German-speaking Greece.

The bulk of the Irish race really lived in the closest contact with the traditions of the past and the national life of nearly eighteen hundred years, until the beginning of this century. Not only so, but during the whole of the dark Penal times they produced amongst themselves a most vigorous literary development. Their schoolmasters and wealthy farmers, unwearied scribes, produced innumerable manuscripts in beautiful writing, each letter separated from another as in Greek, transcripts both of the ancient literature of their sires and of the more modern literature produced by themselves. Until the beginning of the present century there was no county, no barony, and, I may almost say, no townland which did not boast of an Irish poet, the people's representative of those ancient bards who died out with the extirpation of the great Milesian families. The literary activity of even the eighteenth century among the Gaels was very great, not in the South alone, but also in Ulster—the number of poets it produced was something astonishing. It did not, however, produce many works in Gaelic prose, but it propagated translations of many pieces from the French, Latin, Spanish, and English. Every well-to-do farmer could read and write Irish, and many of them could understand even archaic Irish. I have myself heard persons reciting the poems of Donogha More O'Daly, Abbot of Boyle, in Roscommon, who died sixty years before Chaucer was born. To this very day the people have a word for archaic Irish, which is much the same as though Chaucer's poems were handed down amongst the English peasantry, but required a special training to understand. This training, however, nearly every one of fair education during the Penal times possessed, nor did they begin to lose their Irish training and knowledge until after the establishment of Maynooth and the rise of O'Connell. These

two events made an end of the Gaelicism of
the Gaelic race, although a great number of
poets and scribes existed even down to the
forties and fifties of the present century, and
a few may linger on yet in remote localities.
But it may be said, roughly speaking, that the
ancient Gaelic civilisation died with O'Connell,
largely, I am afraid, owing to his example
and his neglect of inculcating the necessity of
keeping alive racial customs, language, and
traditions, in which with the one notable
exception of our scholarly idealist, Smith
O'Brien, he has been followed until a year
ago by almost every leader of the Irish
race.

Thomas Davis and his brilliant band of
Young Irelanders came just at the dividing
of the line, and tried to give to Ireland a new
literature in English to replace the literature
which was just being discarded. It succeeded
and it did not succeed. It was a most brilliant
effort, but the old bark had been too recently
stripped off the Irish tree, and the trunk
could not take as it might have done to a
fresh one. It was a new departure, and at
first produced a violent effect. Yet in the
long run it failed to properly leaven our

peasantry who might, perhaps, have been reached upon other lines. I say they *might* have been reached upon other lines because it is quite certain that even well on into the beginning of this century, Irish poor scholars and schoolmasters used to gain the greatest favour and applause by reading out manuscripts in the people's houses at night, some of which manuscripts had an antiquity of a couple of hundred years or more behind them, and which, when they got illegible from age, were always recopied. The Irish peasantry at that time were all to some extent cultured men, and many of the better off ones were scholars and poets. What have we now left of all that? Scarcely a trace. Many of them read newspapers indeed, but who reads, much less recites, an epic poem, or chants an elegiac or even a hymn?

Wherever Irish throughout Ireland continued to be spoken, there the ancient MSS. continued to be read, there the epics of Cuchullain, Conor MacNessa, Déirdre, Finn, Oscar, and Ossian continued to be told, and there poetry and music held sway. Some people may think I am exaggerating in asserting that such a state of things existed down to the present century, but it is no exaggeration. I have myself spoken with men from Cavan and Tyrone who spoke excellent Irish. Carleton's stories bear witness to the prevalence of the Irish language and traditions in Ulster when he began to write. My friend Mr. Lloyd has found numbers in Antrim who spoke good Irish. And, as for Leinster, my friend Mr. Cleaver informed me that when he lived in Wicklow a man came by from the County Carlow in search of work who could not speak a word of English. Old labourers from Connacht, who used to go to reap the harvest in England and take shipping at Drogheda, told me that at that time, fifty years ago, Irish was spoken by every one round that town. I have met an old man in Wicklow, not twenty miles from Dublin, whose parents always repeated the Rosary in Irish. My friend Father O'Growny, who has done and is doing so much for the Irish language and literature at Maynooth, tells me that there, within twenty miles of Dublin, are three old people who still speak Irish. O'Curry found people within seven miles of Dublin city who had never heard English in their youth at all, except from the car-drivers of the great town. I gave an old man in the street who begged from me, a penny, only a few days ago, saying, " *Sin pighin agad*," and when he answered in Irish I asked him where he was from, and he said from *Newna* (*n' Eamhain*), *i.e.*, Navan. Last year I was in Canada and out hunting with some Red Indians, and we spent a night in the last white man's house in the last settlement on the brink of the primeval forest ; and judging from a peculiarly Hibernian physiognomy that the man was Irish, I addressed him in Gaelic, and to the intense astonishment both of whites and Indians we entered into a conversation which none of them understood ; and it turned out that he was from within three miles of Kilkenny, and had been forty years in that country without forgetting the language he had spoken as a child, and I, although from the centre of Connacht, understood him perfectly. When my father was a young boy in the county Leitrim, not far from Longford, he seldom heard the farm labourers and tenants speak anything but Irish amongst themselves. So much for Ulster and Leinster, but Connacht and Munster were until quite recently completely Gaelic. In fact, I may venture to say,

that, up to the beginning of the present century, neither man, woman, nor child of the
Gaelic race, either of high blood or low blood,
existed in Ireland who did not either speak
Irish or understand it. But within the last
ninety years we have, with an unparalleled
frivolity, deliberately thrown away our birthright and Anglicised ourselves. None of the
children of those people of whom I have
spoken know Irish, and the race will from
henceforth be changed ; for as Monsieur
Jubainville says of the influence of Rome
upon Gaul, England " has definitely conquered us, she has even imposed upon us her
language, that is to say, the form of our
thoughts during every instant of our existence." It is curious that those who most fear
West Britainism have so eagerly consented to
imposing upon the Irish race what, according
to Jubainville, who in common with all the
great scholars of the continent, seems to regret
it very much, is " the form of our thoughts
during every instant of our existence."

So much for the greatest stroke of all in
our Anglicisation, the loss of our language. I
have often heard people thank God that if
the English gave us nothing else they gave

us at least their language. In this way they put a bold face upon the matter, and pretend that the Irish language is not worth knowing, and has no literature. But the Irish language *is* worth knowing, or why would the greatest philologists of Germany, France, and Italy be emulously studying it, and it *does* possess a literature, or why would a German savant have made the calculation that the books written in Irish between the eleventh and seventeenth centuries, and still extant, would fill a thousand octavo volumes.

I have no hesitation at all in saying that every Irish-feeling Irishman, who hates the reproach of West-Britonism, should set himself to encourage the efforts which are being made to keep alive our once great national tongue. The losing of it is our greatest blow, and the sorest stroke that the rapid Anglicisation of Ireland has inflicted upon us. In order to de-Anglicise ourselves we must at once arrest the decay of the language. We must bring pressure upon our politicians not to snuff it out by their tacit discouragement merely because they do not happen themselves to understand it. We must arouse some spark of patriotic inspiration among the peasantry who still use the language, and put an end to the shameful state of feeling—a thousand-tongued reproach to our leaders and statesmen—which makes young men and women blush and hang their heads when overheard speaking their own language.[1] Maynooth has at last come splendidly to the

[1] As an instance of this, I mention the case of a young man I met on the road coming from the fair of Tuam, some ten miles away. I saluted him in Irish, and he answered me in English. "Don't you speak Irish," said I. "Well, I declare to God, sir," he said, "my father and mother hasn't a word of English, but still, I don't speak Irish." This was absolutely true for him. There are thousands upon thousands of houses all over Ireland to-day where the old people invariably use Irish in addressing the children, and the children as invariably answer in English, the children understanding Irish but not speaking it, the parents understanding their children's English but unable to use it themselves. In a great many cases, I should almost say most, the children are not conscious of the existence of two languages. I remember asking a gossoon a couple of miles west of Ballaghaderreen in the Co. Mayo, some questions in Irish and he answered them in English. At last I said to him, "*Nach labhrann tu Gaedheilg?*" (*i.e.*, "Don't you speak Irish?") and his answer was, "And isn't it Irish I'm spaking?" "No *a-chuisle*," said I, "it's not Irish you're speaking, but English." "Well then," said he, "that's how I spoke it ever"! He was quite unconscious

front, and it is now incumbent upon every clerical student to attend lectures in the Irish language and history during the first three years of his course. But in order to keep . the Irish language alive where it is still spoken —which is the utmost we can at present aspire to—nothing less than a house-to-house visitation and exhortation of the people themselves will do, something—though with a very different purpose—analogous to the procedure that James Stephens adopted throughout Ireland when he found her like a corpse on the dissecting table. This and some system of giving medals or badges of honour to every family who will guarantee that they have always spoken Irish amongst themselves during

that I was addressing him in one language and he answering in another. On a different occasion I spoke Irish to a little girl in a house near Kilfree Junction, Co. Sligo, into which I went while waiting for a train. The girl answered me in Irish until her brother came in. "Arrah now, Mary," said he, with what was intended to be a most bitter sneer; "and isn't that a credit to you!" And poor Mary—whom I had with difficulty persuaded to begin — immediately hung her head and changed to English. This is going on from Malin Head to Galway, and from Galway to Waterford, with the exception possibly of a few spots in Donegal and Kerry, where the people are wiser and more national.

the year. But, unfortunately, distracted as we are and torn by contending factions, it is impossible to find either men or money to carry out this simple remedy, although to a dispassionate foreigner—to a Zeuss, Jubainville, Zimmer, Kuno Meyer, Windisch, or Ascoli, and the rest—this is of greater importance than whether Mr. Redmond or Mr. MacCarthy lead the largest wing of the Irish party for the moment, or Mr. So-and-So succeed with his election petition. To a person taking a bird's-eye view of the situation a hundred or five hundred years hence, believe me, it will also appear of greater importance than any mere temporary wrangle, but, unhappily, our countrymen cannot be brought to see this.

We can, however, insist, and we *shall* insist if Home Rule be carried, that the Irish language, which so many foreign scholars of the first calibre find so worthy of study, shall be placed on a par with—or even above—Greek, Latin, and modern languages, in all examinations held under the Irish Government. We can also insist, and we *shall* insist, that in those baronies where the children speak Irish, Irish shall be taught, and that Irish-speaking schoolmasters, petty sessions clerks, and even magistrates be appointed in Irish-speaking districts. If all this were done, it should not be very difficult, with the aid of the foremost foreign scholars, to bring about a tone of thought which would make it disgraceful for an educated Irishman—especially of the old Celtic race, MacDermotts, O'Conors, O'Sullivans, MacCarthys, O'Neills—to be ignorant of his own language—would make it at least as disgraceful as for an educated Jew to be quite ignorant of Hebrew.

We find the decay of our language faithfully reflected in the decay of our surnames. In Celtic times a great proof of the powers of assimilation which the Irish nation possessed, was the fact that so many of the great Norman and English nobles lived like the native chiefs and took Irish names. In this way the De Bourgos of Connacht became MacWilliams, of which clan again some minor branches became MacPhilpins, MacGibbons, and Mac-Raymonds. The Birminghams of Connacht took the name of MacFeóiris, the Stauntons became MacAveelys, the Nangles Mac-Costellos ; the Prendergasts of Mayo became MacMaurices, the De Courcys became Mac

Patricks, the Bissetts of Antrim became MacEóins, and so on. Roughly speaking, it may be said that most of the English and Norman families outside of the Pale were Irish in name and manners from the beginning of the fourteenth to the middle of the seventeenth century.

In 1465 an Act was passed by the Parliament of the English Pale that all Irishmen inside the Pale should take an English name "of one towne as Sutton, Chester, Trym, Skryne, Corke, Kinsale ; or colour, as white, black, brown ; or art or science, as smith or carpenter ; or office, as cooke, butler ; and that he and his issue shall use this name" or forfeit all his goods. A great number of the lesser families complied with this typically English ordinance ; but the greater ones— the MacMurroghs, O'Tooles, O'Byrnes, O'Nolans, O'Mores, O'Ryans, O'Conor Falys, O'Kellys, &c. — refused, and never did change their names. A hundred and thirty years later we find Spenser, the poet, advocating the renewal of this statute. By doing this, says Spenser, "they shall in time learne quite to forget the Irish nation. And herewithal," he says, "would I also wish the

O's and Macs which the heads of septs have
taken to their names to be utterly forbidden
and extinguished, for that the same being an
ordinance (as some say) first made by O'Brien
(Ɔrian boɲúina) for the strengthening of the
Irish, the abrogation thereof will as much
enfeeble them." It was, however, only after
Aughrim and the Boyne that Irish names
began to be changed in great numbers, and
O'Conors to become " Conyers," O'Reillys
" Ridleys," O'Donnells " Daniels," O'Sullivans
" Silvans," MacCarthys " Carters," and so
on.

But it is the last sixty years that have made
most havoc with our Milesian names. It
seemed as if the people were possessed with a
mania for changing them to something—anything at all, only to get rid of the Milesian
sound. " Why," said O'Connell, once talking
to a mass-meeting of Lord Chancellor Sugden,
" you wouldn't call a decent pig Sugden." Yet
he never uttered a word of remonstrance at
the O'Lahiffs, O'Brollahans, and MacRorys
becoming under his eyes Guthrys, Bradleys,
and Rogerses. It is more than a little curious,
and a very bad augury for the future independence of Ireland, that men of education and

intelligence like Carleton the novelist, or
Hardiman, author of the "History of Galway" and the "Irish Minstrelsy," should
have changed their Milesian names, one from
that of O'Cairellan, who was ancient chief of
Clandermot, the other from the well-known
name of O'Hargadain. In Connacht alone I
know scores of Gatelys, Sextons, Baldwins,
Foxes, Coxes, Footes, Greenes, Keatings, who
are really O'Gatlies, O'Sesnans, O'Mulligans,
O'Shanahans, MacGillacullys, O'Trehys,
O'Honeens, and O'Keateys. The O'Hennesys
are Harringtons, the O'Kinsellaghs, Kingsleys
and Tinslys, the O'Feehillys Pickleys, and so
on. O'Donovan, writing in 1862, gives a list
of names which had recently been changed in
the neighbourhood of Cootehill, Co. Cavan.
These Irish names of MacNebo, MacIntyre,
MacGilroy, MacTernan, MacCorry, MacOscar,
MacBrehon, O'Clery, Murtagh, O'Drum, &c.,
were becoming, or had become, Victory, Vic-
toria, Callwell, Freeman, King, Nugent, Gil
man, Leonard, Godwin, Goodwin, Smyth,
Golderich, Golding, Masterton, Lind, Crosby,
Grosby, Crosse, Corry, Cosgrove, Judge,
Brabacy, Brabazon, Clarke, Clerkin, Cun-
ningham, Drummond, Tackit, Sexton, and

Mortimer [1] — not a bad attempt at West-Britonising for one little town !

Numbers of people, again, like Mr. Davitt or Mr. Hennessy, drop the O and Mac which

[1] The following are a few instances out of hundreds of the monstrous transmographying of Gaelic names into English. The Gillespies (Giolla-Easbuig, *i.e.*, Bishop's servant) are Archbolds or Bishops. The Mackays (Mac Aodha, *i.e.*, son of Ae or Hugh) are Hughes. The Mac Reevys or Mac Culreevys (Mac Cùil-Riabhaigh, *i.e.*, son of the grey poll) are Grays. The Mac Eóchagains instead of being all Gahagans or Geoghegans have—some of them — deformed their name into the monstrosity of Goggin. The Mac Feeachrys (Mac Fhiachraidh) are Vickors or even Hunters. The Mac Feehalys are often Fieldings. Mac Gilleesa (Mac Giolla Iosa, *i.e.*, sons of Jesus' devotee) are either Gillespie or Giles. The Mac Gillamurrys (Mac Giolla-Mhuire, *i.e.*, son of the Virgin's devotee) is often made Marmion, sometimes more correctly Macilmurray or Mac Ilmurry. Mac Gillamerry (Mac Giolla Meidhre, *i.e.*, son of the servant of merriment) is Anglicised Merryman. Mac Gillaree (Mac Giolla-righ, *i.e.*, son of the king's servant) is very often made King, but sometimes pretty correctly Mac Gilroy or Mao Ilroy— thus the Connemara people have made Kingston of the village of Ballyconry, because the *ry* or *righ* means a king. The Mac Irs, sons of Ir, earliest coloniser of Ireland, have, by some confusion with *geirr*, the genitive of *gearr*, "short," become Shorts or Shortalls, but sometimes, less corruptly, Kerrs. The honourable name of Mac Rannell (Mac Raghnaill) is now seldom met with in

properly belong to their names ; others, without actually changing them, metamorphose
their names, as we have seen, into every possible form. I was told in America that the first

any other form than that of Reynolds. The Mac Sorarans
(Mac Samhradháin, the clan or tribe name of the Mac
Gaurans or Mac Governs) have become Somers, through
some fancied etymology with the word *samhradh*. The
Mac Sorleys (Mac Samharlaigh) are often Shirleys. The
honourable and poetic race of Mac-an-bháirds (sons of the
bard) are now Wards to a man. The Mac-intleevys
(Mac an tsléibhe, *i.e.*, sons of the mountain) are Levys
or Dunlevys. The Macintaggarts (Mac an tsagairt, *i.e.*,
son of the priest) are now Priestmans, or occasionally, I
do not know why, Segraves. The Macgintys (Mac an
tsaoi, *i.e.*, son of the sage) are very often Nobles. The
Macinteers (Mac an tsaoir, *i.e.*, son of the carpenter)
instead of being made MacIntyre as the Scots always
have it, are in Ireland Carpenters or Wrights, or—because *saor* means "free" as well as Carpenter—Frees and
Freemans. Many of the O'Hagans (O h-Aodhgáin) are
now Fagans, and even Dickens's Fagan the Jew has not
put a stop to the hideous transformation. The O'Hillans
(Mac Ui Iollain, *i.e.*, sons of Illan, a great name in Irish
romance) have become Hylands or Whelans. It would
be tedious to go through all the well-known names that
immediately occur to one as thus suffering ; suffice it to
say, that the O'Heas became Hayses, the O'Queenahans,
Mosses, Mossmans, and Kinahans, the O'Longans Longs,
the O'Naghtens Nortons, the O'Reardons Salmons,
the O'Shanahans Foxes, and so on *ad infinitum*.

Chauncey who ever came out there was an
O'Shaughnessy, who went to, I think, Mary-
land, in the middle of the last century, and
who had twelve sons, who called themselves
Chauncey, and from whom most of or all the
Chaunceys in America are descended. I know
people who have translated their names within the last ten years. This vile habit is going
on with almost unabated vigour, and nobody
has ever raised a protest against it. Out of
the many hundreds of O'Byrnes—offshoots of
the great Wicklow chieftains—in the city of
New York, only four have retained that name ;
all the rest have taken the Scotch name of
Burns. I have this information from two of
the remaining four, both friends of my own,
and both splendid Gaelic scholars, though
from opposite ends of Ireland, Donegal and
Waterford. Of two brothers of whom I was
lately told, though I do not know them per-
sonally, one is an O'Gara, and still condescends
to remain connected with the patron of the
Four Masters and a thousand years of a glorious
past, whilst the other (through some etymo-
logical confusion with the word Caraim,
which means " I love ") calls himself Mr.
Love ! Another brother remains a Brehony,

thus showing his descent from one of the very highest and most honourable titles in Ireland—a Brehon, law-giver and poet ; the other brother is John Judge. In fact, hundreds of thousands of Irishmen prefer to drop their honourable Milesian names, and call themselves Groggins or Duggan, or Higgins or Guthry, or any other beastly name, in preference to the surnames of warriors, saints, and poets ; and the melancholy part of it is, that not one single word of warning or remonstrance has been raised, as far as I am aware, against this colossal cringing either by the Irish public press or public men.

With our Irish Christian names the case is nearly as bad. Where are now all the fine old Irish Christian names of both men and women which were in vogue even a hundred years ago ? They have been discarded as unclean things, not because they were ugly in themselves or inharmonious, but simply because they were not English. No man is now christened by a Gaelic name, " nor no woman neither." Such common Irish Christian names as Conn, Cairbre, Farfeasa, Teig, Diarmuid, Kian, Cuan, Ae, Art, Mahon, Eochaidh, Fearflatha, Cathan, Rory, Coll, Lochlainn,

Cathal, Lughaidh, Turlough, Éamon, Randal, Niall, Sorley, and Conor, are now extinct or nearly so. Donough and Murrough survive in the O'Brien family. Angus, Manus, Fergal, and Felim are now hardly known. The man whom you call Diarmuid when you speak Irish, a low, pernicious, un-Irish, detestable custom, begot by slavery, propagated by cringing, and fostered by flunkeyism, forces you to call Jeremiah when you speak English, or as a concession, Darby. In like manner, the indigenous Teig is West-Britonised into Thaddeus or Thady, for no earthly reason than that both begin with a T. Donough is Denis, Cahal is Charles, Murtagh and Murough are Mortimer, Dómhnall is Daniel, Partholan, the name of the earliest coloniser of Ireland, is Bartholomew or Batty,[1] Eoghan (Owen) is frequently Eugene, and our own O'Curry, though he plucked up courage to prefix the O to his name in later life, never discarded the Eugene, which, however, is far from being a monstrosity like most of our West-Britonised names ; Félim is Felix, Fin-

[1] It is questionable, however, whether Partholan as a modern Christian name is not itself an Irishised form of Bartholomew.

ghin (Finneen) is Florence, Conor is Corney, Turlough is Terence, Éamon is Edmond or Neddy, and so on. In fact, of the great wealth of Gaelic Christian names in use a century or two ago, only Owen, Brian, Cormac, and Patrick seem to have survived in general use.

Nor have our female names fared one bit better; we have discarded them even more ruthlessly than those of our men. Surely Sadhbh (Sive) is a prettier name than Sabina or Sibby, and Nóra than Onny, Honny, or Honour (so translated simply because Nóra sounds like *onóir*, the Irish for "honour"); surely Una is prettier than Winny, which it becomes when West-Britonised. Mève, the great name of the Queen of Connacht who led the famous cattle spoiling of Cuailgne, celebrated in the greatest Irish epic, is at least as pretty as Maud, which it becomes when Anglicised, and Eibhlin (Eileen) is prettier than Ellen or Elinor. Aoife (Eefy), Sighle (Sheela), Móirin (Moreen), Nuala and Fionnuala (Finnoola), are all beautiful names which were in use until quite recently. Maurya and Anya are still common, but are not indigenous Irish names at all, so that I do not mind their rejection, whilst three other very common ones, Suraha, Shinéad, and Shuwaun, sound so bad in English that I do not very much regret their being translated into Sarah, Jane, and Joan respectively ; but I must put in a plea for the retention of such beautiful words as Eefee, Oona, Eileen, Mève, Sive, and Nuala. Of all the beautiful Christian names of women which were in use a century or two ago Brighid (Breed), under the ugly form of Bridget, or still worse, of Biddy, and Eiblin under the form of Eveleen, and perhaps Norah, seem to be the only survivals, and they are becoming rarer. I *do* think that the time has now come to make a vigorous protest against this continued West-Briton-ising of ourselves, and that our people ought to have a word in season addressed to them by their leaders which will stop them from translating their Milesian surnames into hideous Saxon, and help to introduce Irish instead of English Christian names. As long as the Irish nation goes on as it is doing I cannot have much hope of its ultimately taking its place amongst the nations of the earth, for if it does, it will have proceeded upon different lines from every other nationality that God ever created. I hope that we shall never be satisfied either as individuals or as a society as long as the Brehonys call themselves Judges, the Clan Govern call themselves Smiths, and the O'Reardons Salmons, as long as our boys are called Dan and Jeremiah instead of Donal and Diarmuid, and our girls Honny, Winny, and Ellen instead of Nóra, Una, and Eileen.

Our topographical nomenclature too—as we may now be prepared to expect—has been also shamefully corrupted to suit English ears ; but unfortunately the difficulties attendant upon a realteration of our place-names to their proper forms are very great, nor do I mean to go into this question now, for it is one so long and so difficult that it would require a lecture, or rather a series of. lectures to itself. Suffice it to say, that many of the best-known names in our history and annals have become almost wholly unrecognisable, through the ignorant West-Britonising of them. The unfortunate natives of the eighteenth century allowed all kinds of havoc to be played with even their best-known names. For example the river Feóir they allowed to be turned permanently into the Nore, which happened this way. Some Englishman, asking the name of the river, was told that it was *An Fheóir*, pronounced In n'yore, because the F when preceded by the definite article *an* is not sounded, so that in his ignorance he mistook the word Feóir for Neóir, and the name has been thus perpetuated. In the same way the great Connacht lake, Loch Corrib, is really Loch Orrib, or rather Loch Orbsen, some Englishman having mistaken the C at the end of loch for the beginning of the next word. Sometimes the Ordnance Survey people make a rough guess at the Irish name and jot down certain English letters almost on chance. Sometimes again they make an Irish word resemble an English one, as in the celebrated Tailtin in Meath, where the great gathering of the nation was held, and, which, to make sure that no national memories should stick to it, has been West-Britonised Telltown.[1] On the whole, our place names have been treated with about the same respect as if they were the names of a savage tribe which had never before been reduced to writing, and with

---

[1] For more information about Tailtin, see an article by me incorporated in the "Rules of the Gaelic Athletic Association," recently published.

about the same intelligence and contempt as vulgar English squatters treat the topographical nomenclature of the Red Indians. These things are now to a certain extent stereotyped, and are difficult at this hour to change, especially where Irish names have been translated into English, like Swinford and Strokestown, or ignored as in Charleville or Midleton. But though it would take the strength and goodwill of an united nation to put our topographical nomenclature on a rational basis like that of Wales and the Scotch Highlands, there is one thing which our Society can do, and that is to insist upon pronouncing our Irish names properly. Why will a certain class of people insist upon getting as far away from the pronunciation of the natives as possible? I remember a Galway gentleman pulling me up severely for speaking of Athenree. "It's not Athenree," he said, "it's called Athenrye." Yet in saying this he simply went out of his way to mispronounce the historic name, which means the "King's ford," and which all the natives call -ree, not -rye.[1] Another instance out of many thousands is my own market

---

[1] In Irish it is Beul-áth-an-righ contracted into B'l'áth-'n-righ, pronounced *Blawn-ree*.

town, Ballagh-ă-derreen, literally, "the way of the oak-wood." Ballach is the same word as in the phrase *Fág a' bealach*, "clear the way," and "derreen" is the diminutive of Derry, an oak-wood. Yet the more "civilised" of the population, perhaps one in fifty, offend one's ears with the frightful jargon Bálla-hád-hereen. Thus Lord Iveagh (Ee-vah) becomes Lord Ivy, and Scana-guala, the old sholder, becomes Shanagolden, and leads you to expect a mine, or at least a furze-covered hill.

I shall not give any more examples of deliberate carelessness, ineptitude, and West-Britonising in our Irish topography, for the instances may be numbered by thousands and thousands. I hope and trust that where it may be done without any great inconvenience a native Irish Government will be induced to provide for the restoration of our place-names on something like a rational basis.

Our music, too, has become Anglicised to an alarming extent. Not only has the national instrument, the harp—which efforts are now being made to revive in the Highlands—become extinct, but even the Irish pipes are threatened with the same fate. In place of

the pipers and fiddlers who, even twenty years
ago, were comparatively common, we are now
in many places menaced by the German band
and the barrel organ. Something should be
done to keep the native pipes and the native
airs amongst us still. If Ireland loses her
music she loses what is, after her Gaelic language and literature, her most valuable and
most characteristic possession. And she is
rapidly losing it. A few years ago all our
travelling fiddlers and pipers could play the
old airs which were then constantly called for,
the *Cúis d'á pléidh*, *Drinaun Dunn*, *Roseen
Dubh*, *Gamhan Geal Bán*, *Eileen-a-roon*,
Shawn O'Dwyer in Glanna, and the rest,
whether gay or plaintive, which have for so
many centuries entranced the Gael. But now
English music-hall ballads and Scotch songs
have gained an enormous place in the reper-
toire of the wandering minstrel, and the
minstrels themselves are becoming fewer and
fewer, and I fear worse and worse. It is difficult to find a remedy for this. I am afraid in
this practical age to go so far as to advocate
the establishment in Cork or Galway of a
small institution in which young and promising pipers might be trained to play all the

Irish airs and sent forth to delight our population ; for I shall be told that this is not a
matter for even an Irish Government to stir
in, though it is certain that many a Government has lavished money on schemes less
pleasant and less useful. For the present,
then, I must be content with hoping that the
revival of our Irish music may go hand in
hand with the revival of Irish ideas and
Celtic modes of thought which our Society is
seeking to bring about, and that people may
be brought to love the purity of *Siúbhail
Siúbhail*, or the fun of the *Moddereen Ruadh*
in preference to "Get Your Hair Cut," or
"Over the Garden Wall," or, even if it is not
asking too much, of "Ta-ra-ra-boom-de-ay."

Our games, too, were in a most grievous
condition until the brave and patriotic men
who started the Gaelic Athletic Association
took in hand their revival. I confess that the
instantaneous and extraordinary success which
attended their efforts when working upon
national lines has filled me with more hope
for the future of Ireland than everything else
put together. I consider the work of the
association in reviving our ancient national
game of caman, or hurling, and Gaelic foot-

ball, has done more for Ireland than all the
speeches of politicians for the last five years.
And it is not alone that that splendid association revived for a time with vigour our national
sports, but it revived also our national recollec-
tions, and the names of the various clubs
through the country have perpetuated the
memory of the great and good men and
martyrs of Ireland. The physique of our
youth has been improved in many of our
counties; they have been taught self-restraint,
and how to obey their captains; they have
been, in many places, weaned from standing
idle in their own roads or street corners; and
not least, they have been introduced to the use
of a thoroughly good and Irish garb. Wherever the warm striped green jersey of the
Gaelic Athletic Association was seen, there
Irish manhood and Irish memories were rapidly
reviving. There torn collars and ugly neck-
ties hanging awry and far better not there at all,
and dirty shirts of bad linen were banished, and
our young hurlers were clad like men and
Irishmen, and not in the shoddy second-hand
suits of Manchester and London shop-boys.
Could not this alteration be carried still
further? Could we not make that jersey

still more popular, and could we not, in places where both garbs are worn, use our influence against English second-hand trousers, generally dirty in front, and hanging in muddy tatters at the heels, and in favour of the cleaner worsted stockings and neat breeches which many of the older generation still wear? Why have we discarded our own comfortable frieze? Why does every man in Connemara wear home-made and home-spun tweed, while in the midland counties we have become too proud for it, though we are not too proud to buy at every fair and market the most incongruous cast-off clothes imported from English cities, and to wear them? Let us, as far as we have any influence, set our faces against this aping of English dress, and encourage our women to spin and our men to wear comfortable frieze suits of their own wool, free from shoddy and humbug. So shall we de-Anglicise Ireland to some purpose, foster a native spirit and a growth of native custom which will form the strongest barrier against English influence and be in the end the surest guarantee of Irish autonomy.

I have now mentioned a few of the principal points on which it would be desirable for us

to move, with a view to de-Anglicising ourselves ; but perhaps the principal point of all I
have taken for granted. That is the necessity
for encouraging the use of Anglo-Irish literature instead of English books, especially
instead of English periodicals. We must set
our face sternly against penny dreadfuls,
shilling shockers, and still more, the garbage
of vulgar English weeklies like *Bow Bells* and
the *Police Intelligence*. Every house should
have a copy of Moore and Davis. In a word,
we must strive to cultivate everything that
is most racial, most smacking of the soil, most
Gaelic, most Irish, because in spite of the little
admixture of Saxon blood in the north-east
corner, this island *is* and will *ever* remain
Celtic at the core, far more Celtic than most
people imagine, because, as I have shown you,
the names of our people are no criterion of
their race. On racial lines, then, we shall
best develop, following the bent of our own
natures ; and, in order to do this, we must
create a strong feeling against West-Britonism,
for it—if we give it the least chance, or show
it the smallest quarter—will overwhelm us
like a flood, and we shall find ourselves toil-
ing painfully behind the English at each step

following the same fashions, only six months behind the English ones ; reading the same books, only months behind them : taking up the same fads, after they have become stale *there*, following *them* in our dress, literature, music, games, and ideas, only a long time after them and a vast way behind. We will become, what, I fear, we are largely at present, a nation of imitators, the Japanese of Western Europe, lost to the power of native initiative and alive only to second-hand assimilation. I do not think I am overrating this danger. We are probably at once the most assimilative and the most sensitive nation in Europe. A lady in Boston said to me that the Irish immigrants had become Americanised on the journey out before ever they landed at Castle Gardens. And when I ventured to regret it, she said, shrewdly, " If they did not at once become Americanised they would not be Irish." I knew fifteen Irish workmen who were working in a haggard in England give up talking Irish amongst themselves because the English farmer laughed at them. And yet O'Connell used to call us the " finest peasantry in Europe." Unfortunately, he took little care that we should remain so.

We must teach ourselves to be less sensitive, we must teach ourselves not to be ashamed of ourselves, because the Gaelic people can never produce its best before the world as long as it remains tied to the apron-strings of another race and another island, waiting for *it* to move before it will venture to take any step itself.

In conclusion, I would earnestly appeal to every one, whether Unionist or Nationalist, who wishes to see the Irish nation produce its best—and surely whatever our politics are we all wish that—to set his face against this constant running to England for our books, literature, music, games, fashions, and ideas. I appeal to every one whatever his politics—for this is no political matter—to do his best to help the Irish race to develop in future upon Irish lines, even at the risk of encouraging national aspirations, because upon Irish lines alone can the Irish race once more become what it was of yore—one of the most original, artistic, literary, and charming peoples of Europe.

UNWIN BROTHERS,

THE GRESHAM PRESS,

CHILWORTH AND LONDON

THE PATRIOT PARLIAMENT

Of 1689, with its Statutes, Rites, and Proceedings.

By THOMAS DAVIS.

Edited, with an Introduction, by the Hon. Sir
CHARLES GAVAN DUFFY, K.C.M.G.

LONDON : T. FISHER UNWIN, Paternoster Square.
DUBLIN : SEALY, BRYERS & WALKER, Middle Abbey Street.
NEW YORK: P. J. KENEDY, Barclay Street.

NOTICES OF THE BRITISH PRESS.

From THE DAILY NEWS.

The remarkable Series of papers on " The Patriot Parliament."

From THE PALL MALL GAZETTE.

The papers are by far the most valuable of Davis's contribution to Irish history. Mr Lecky, in his history, has spoken of them with much admiration, and has adopted many of their conclusions. The account of the Jacobite Parliament which is given by Lord Macaulay has long been generally accepted in England, but we believe that any one who will candidly examine the evidence that is collected by Davis will arrive at the conclusion that this account is seriously misleading.

To many, however, the most attractive part of this little volume will be the introduction which is written by Sir Gavan Duffy. It is a brilliant and powerful indictment of the government of Ireland under the Stuarts. It is impossible to mistake the accent of sincerity that runs through his pages, and very few men have written Irish history with such eloquence and force.

From THE WESTMINSTER GAZETTE.

We have Mr. Lecky's testimony that Davis's account of what he calls the Patriot Parliament is "the best and fullest" he is acquainted with. He has made it clear that Macaulay's condemnation of the Parliament was over coloured.

From NOTES AND QUERIES.

We do not discuss politics, even when upwards of two hundred years intervenes between the then and the now. From the literary point of view, taking into consideration the limitations of a popular book, we have little but praise to give to Davis's " Patriot Parliament." He wrote as a partisan ; but we detect no perversion of facts. Sir Charles Gavan Duffy's introduction is remarkably interesting. Some of our readers will like to put this volume on the shelf where they keep their books of historic reference, for in the appendix is a carefully compiled catalogue of the Lords and Commons of the Parliament of 1689.

From THE TIMES.

A reprint of a politico-historical tract by a writer highly commended by Mr. Lecky, with an appreciative biographical introduction from the pen of a well-known authority on Irish history.

From THE GLOBE.

Mr. Lecky once described Davis's work as "by far the best and fullest account" of the assembly in question, and in reproducing it the Irish Society have earned the thanks of all students of Irish history.

From THE SCOTSMAN.

The work is a valuable and instructive account of the work done by "the Popish Parliament of James II." It is introduced by a paper in which its editor tells all that need be known of Davis, and shows in what respects his account corrects Macaulay. The reissue should be welcome to every one interested in Irish history.

From THE MANCHESTER GUARDIAN.

It is a vigorous and readable paper, and it carries weight with it.

From THE NEWCASTLE CHRONICLE.

Sir Charles Gavan Duffy's introduction extends to nearly one hundred pages, and traces in bold and rapid lines the history of Ireland under the Stuarts. It is written with that ease, lucidity, and decision which marks the style of Davis's colleague of fifty years ago, who now does this service to the history of his country and to the memory of his friend.

From THE SCOTTISH LEADER.

It would not have been easy indeed to make a better opening of such a series as this aspires to be. "The Patriotic Parliament" is only a characteristic fragment of the work of one of Ireland's most notable heroes, and it is also a contribution of real merit to Irish history. A perusal of this little book will fully justify Mr. Lecky's praise of the skill and industry displayed by Davis, at the same time that it will fill one with a kind of amused admiration of the fervid and somewhat youthful enthusiasm of the "Young Ireland" of 1845.

From THE FREEMAN.

The Irish Parliament of 1690 has been seriously maligned by Macaulay, Froude, Ingram, and others. This is a vindication, and the work of an Irish Protestant. The introduction by Sir Charles Gavan Duffy is very vividly written and gives a view of the colonisation of Ulster of a very serious character. We have not space for the story as given here, but we commend, it to our readers who desire to understand the springs of Irish discontent.

From THE BAPTIST.

To impartial students of history Davis's work will be indispensable.

From THE METHODIST TIMES.

This humble-looking little book marks an era. Sir Charles Duffy has prefixed an introduction in which he tells once more the long story of Ireland's wrongs. The perusal of it makes one feel that England will never lay aside her prejudices and look at Irish questions as she looks at Italian or Russian questions. After Sir C. G. Duffy's introduction comes Thomas Davis's modest preface. It fills five pages; it was written just fifty years ago. It is altogether admirable in tone and sentiment.

From THE UNIVERSE.

We are of opinion that the issue of this new library will tend to place the position of our country more fairly before the public, and will foster a much-wanted knowledge of Ireland, its requirements and its failings, amongst our own people We bid the patriotic venture most heartily welcome.

As a necessity, this opening book is identified with Thomas Davis—not by any means that it is the best specimen of his thought or writing—as in some sort acting as a hyphen between his era and ours—the era of glorious promise and that of partial fruition. Sir Gavan Duffy—thanks that he still survives—supplies a masterly introduction, which to us is the kernel of the volume.

From THE CATHOLIC TIMES.

Not the least of the many services which Sir Charles Gavan Duffy's prolific pen has rendered to the country which gave him birth, and which he has long loved and served with patriotic devotion, is the interesting historical introduction he has prefixed to Thomas Davis's " Patriotic Parliament." The mind of the statesman, the heart of the patriot, and the hand of the practised politician are strikingly evident on every page of this powerful polemic.

From THE WEEKLY REGISTER.

We are, it may be hoped, at the beginning of a better time. Along with the publications of the Irish Literary Society, which have just begun so well with " The Patriotic Parliament of 1689," the joint work of Thomas Davis and Gavan Duffy, the twin brethren of modern literature in Ireland, may we see also many a publication by the Irish clergy of such books as the two we have named, and the volumes published some years ago by the present Coadjutor-Bishop for Kildare and Leighlin.

From THE COLONIES AND INDIA.

The book before us is one which no student of Irish history can well be without, for it discloses in what is no doubt the true light the character of the Catholic Parliament of James II.

From THE WEEKLY DESPATCH.

The volume, a very graphic account of the " Patriot Parliament" of 1689, written by Thomas Davis, the Irish patriot of two generations back, is an interesting and very instructive narrative, correcting the slanders and false statements of Macaulay and other English historians, and showing how just, and even how tolerant of Protestant aliens, Irish Catholics could be in the short time allowed to them, more than a hundred years before Grattan's Parliament came into existence, for experimenting in Home Rule. But the most readable portion of the volume is the long introduction supplied by the editor, Sir Charles Gavan Duffy, who here succinctly reminds us of some of the wrongs inflicted on his fellow-countrymen and fellow-religionists in the old days, and not yet redressed.

From THE WEEKLY SUN.

There ought to be many such books in circulation in England and Ireland, and I hope that this volume will run through many editions. Ignorance has been the bane of the two countries hitherto. Books like "The Irish Parliament under James II." will go far to cement that feeling of friendship by showing the people of this country how erroneous their preconceived opinions of the character of the Irish people have been.

From THE FREEMAN'S JOURNAL.

Though written fifty years ago, it is as much alive with lessons for the hour as any composition of recent date. The introduction is in itself a most valuable summary of the story of Ireland during the Stuart period. Together with Davis's work it forms a book of which no student of Irish history or Irish politics can afford to remain in ignorance.

From THE LYCEUM.

Sir Charles Gavan Duffy in his Introduction gives us a sketch of the times immediately preceding the 1689 Parliament, beginning with the Plantation of Ulster under James I. Step by step he traces the course of events through the dark period of Cromwell's campaigns, through the reign of Charles II., with his lack of good faith and honour in his dealings with Ireland, down to the time when James, a fugitive from his own country and in peril of his life, landed on the shores of Ireland and summoned a Parliament of his Irish subjects. Davis's writings on this Parliament and his ample vindication of it from the contumely and abuse so freely bestowed on it, have now, for the first time, been collected together and given to the reading world as a connected whole. It is a book to be closely studied as throwing a bright and instructive light on a dark and much misrepresented portion of Irish history.

From THE DUBLIN DAILY INDEPENDENT.

To Sir Charles Gavan Duffy this work must have been much of a labour of love. Of that company of devoted Irishmen who had gathered together in Dublin nigh fifty years ago—he alone survives with one other, a busy philanthropist in a southern city who has enhanced the beauty of our national ballads and endeared himself to his countrymen thereby. The coming home of Gavan Duffy to renew the work of his early manhood after half a century of exile is an interesting incident. The young fresh revival in Irish literature in its connection with these few fine old men is as the return of the Son of Cool to the few remaining old Fians who kept true to the traditions of their youth in the heart of the wooded hills of Connaught. It is the proof that their fond hopes cannot be for ever unfulfilled. Sharing with Sir Charles Gavan Duffy the *kudos* of editing the New Library were two men—not unknown to their countrymen. One of them, as *An Chraoibhin Aoibhinn*, has laboured earnestly and well to resuscitate an interest in the purely Gaelic side of Irish literature—Dr. Douglas Hyde. The other, recognising that Thomas Davis's influence is of that peculiar kind rather bequeathed than withdrawn, has gone forth zealously to the endeavour of making Thomas Davis understanded of the people, and with confidence to Mr. T. W. Rolleston may be entrusted the gathering up the fragments that remain—that nothing be lost—of those who brought a new soul into Erinn.

From THE DUBLIN EVENING TELEGRAPH.
An able work, by Thomas Davis, edited by Sir Charles Gavan Duffy, with a magnificent essay on the Stuart and Cromwell period. That we should get such a jewel as this first volume, such a thing of beauty for a shilling, is little short of a marvel.

From THE CORK HERALD.
It might be said, without exaggeration, that the appearance of this work—the forerunner as it is of a series in which Irish life, Irish genius, and Irish character will be represented—constitutes an event of no ordinary importance in Irish history. It is the outcome of a desire and a want which have been long felt that the Irish people should know accurately and intimately everything connected with the past history of their country, with its literature, its music, its antiquities, and its art. The same idea which is now taking visible shape, presented itself to the minds of the leaders of the Young Ireland movement fifty years ago, when a series of little books was published which have since been the companions, the inspiration, and the delight of two generations of Irishmen at home and abroad. There are few Irishmen who have not at one time or another received a potent intellectual stimulus from the writings of Davis or Duffy, Mitchell or M'Nevin. We do not err, therefore, when we say that great possibilities lie hidden in this new movement.

LONDON :
T. FISHER UNWIN, PATERNOSTER SQUARE, E.C.

WORKS by DOUGLAS HYDE, LL.D. (An Chraoibhin Aoibhinn).

"LEABHAR SGEULUIGHEACHTA."

viii—261 *pp.*, 8*vo.* *Price* 5/-. *Gill & Son, O'Connell Street, Dublin.*

Containing some sixteen Folk Tales, Riddles, Ranns, &c., in Irish, with copious Notes on the Pronunciation, Vocabulary, and Dialect.

"The multitude of characteristic idioms and of those charmingly expressive turns of speech which one meets with daily among the peasantry is so great as to make the work a perfect treasure-house of rich jewels of thought. . . . Dr. Hyde deserves well, not only of his country, but of all scientific investigators and philologists."—*Freeman's Journal.*

"This is the most noteworthy addition that has been made for nearly a century to modern Gaelic literature."—*Chicago Citizen.*

"His collection of Irish Gaelic Folk Stories is the fruit of years of pious work. He has travelled into every corner of Ireland where the old tongue still lingers, gathering from the mouths of the Irish-speaking peasants the olden stories that linger among them."—*Nation.*

"BESIDE THE FIRE."

lviii—204 *pp., large* 8*vo.* *Price* 7/6. *David Nutt, Strand, London.*

Containing Folk Tales and Fairy Stories in Irish and English, collected from the mouths of the peasantry. With Introduction and Notes, and additional Notes by ALFRED NUTT.

"Any reader conversant with the subject will at once recognise the fact that this book is distinctly the most valuable contribution that has ever been made to Irish Folk-lore. It would be hardly an exaggeration to say that it is the only work in that particular department that is trustworthy in its details and scientific in its treatment."—*Nature.*

"We may say that Dr. Hyde's is the first [collection of Irish Folk-lore] which has been presented in a form entirely satisfactory to the scientific folk-lorist. . . . Few men know the living Gaelic tongue so well as Dr. Hyde, and he has made it his object to give these fragments of Gaelic tradition exactly as he gathered them from the lips of the peasantry, and with all the collateral information that the scientific investigator can require. The result is certainly one of the most interesting and entertaining books of Folk-lore that it has ever been our good fortune to come across."—*The Speaker.*

"Perhaps the most interesting part of Dr. Hyde's collection of Irish tales, 'Beside the Fire,' is his Introduction."—*Saturday Review.*

"We trust that his warning, though late, is not given in vain, and that a whole literature will not be allowed to die or to become a fossil in the studies of the Dryasdusts."—*Daily News leading article.*

"COIS NA TEINEADH."

60 *pp., large* 8*vo.* *Price* 1/6. *Gill & Son, O'Connell Street, Dublin.*

Containing six Folk Stories in Irish, reprinted from the last volume. With Additional Notes, &c.

CONTES IRLANDAIS.

Being Extracts from the untranslated portion of the "Leabhar Sgeuluigheachta," translated into French by M. GEORGES DOTTIN, with the original Irish text in Roman letters as arranged by Monsieur DOTTIN on the opposite page.

70 *pp.*, 4*to.* *Price* **7/6.** *Gill & Son, O'Connell Street, Dublin.*

ABHRÁIN GRÁDH;

OR,

LOVE SONGS OF CONNACHT.

Containing 45 Poems collected from the mouths of Connacht peasantry or from modern manuscripts, now for the first time collected, translated, and published, with metrical and literal versions in English on one side of the page and the Irish text on the other, with Notes, Anecdotes, and much Illustrative matter.

160 *pp.*, 8*vo.* *Price* **2/6** *net.* *T. Fisher Unwin, Paternoster Buildings, and Gill & Son, Upper O'Connell Street, Dublin.*

"In these Connaught Love Songs Dr. Hyde has made, whether in verse or prose, the best transcript of Celtic poetry into English that we have yet had. So much of the magic, so much of the local colour, the native grace, the idiom of the Irish as he has given, one had thought it impossible to give."—ERNEST RHYS, *in the Academy, Oct.* 13*th*, 1893.

"We cannot too cordially commend to ethnologists and Gaelic antiquarians these relics of Irish Folk Songs collected with so much industry and devotion by Dr. Hyde."—*The Times, July* 20*th*, 1893.

"The price of this valuable and delightful work is only half-a-crown, and it should be welcomed by several classes of readers. The folklorists of course will pounce on it, but folk-lorists are a very small public and despised of men. Still less numerous are students of the Irish language, who here find what they need, the Erse poetry on the left page, the literal translation on the right. . . . There remains the class of English readers of poetry, and to them the 'Love Songs of Connacht' may be warmly recommended."—*From the Daily News leading article, Sept. 1st,* 1893.

"No one who has examined Dr. Hyde's previous work can fail to see that he combines two gifts, the conjunction of which is rarely met with in one man; he adds to the knowledge, the love of accuracy, and the scientific spirit of a modern scholar that sense of the *form,* and love of the *spirit* of his material which belongs to the creative far more than to the critical mind. And if such praise seems to any reader excessive, let him examine for himself the 'Fourth Chapter of the Songs of Connacht.'"
—*From the Speaker, July* 15*th*, 1893.

"Every page deserves some quotation. . . . Accompanying the poems is the enchanting commentary of Dr. Hyde; he tells of the old folk from whose lips, of the old manuscripts, from whose pages he took his songs. He is philosophical, historical, scientific, at need. . . . The reader will reflect that were these poems, or poems a thousand times less good in Greek or Latin, old French, or old German, or songs of Russia or Roumania, many a learned man, many a lover of poetry, would be keen to edit, criticise, proclaim them."—*From the Daily Chronicle, Aug.* 21*st*, 1893.

The Reformer's
Book=Shelf.

Large crown 8vo, cloth, **3s. 6d.** *each.*

I.

The English Peasant: His Past and
Present. By RICHARD HEATH.

II.

The Labour Movement. By L. T.
HOBHOUSE, M.A. Preface by R. B. HALDANE,
M.P.

III.

Sixty Years of an Agitator's Life:
The Third and Cheaper Edition of GEO. JACOB HOLY-
OAKE'S Autobiography. 2 vols. With Portrait by
WALTER SICKERT.

IV.

Bamford's Passages in the Life of
a Radical. Edited, and with an Introduction, by
HENRY DUNCKLEY ("VERAX"). 2 vols.

LONDON:

T. FISHER UNWIN, PATERNOSTER SQUARE, E.C.

IRISH LITERATURE.

LOVE SONGS OF IRELAND. Collected and Edited by KATHARINE TYNAN. Fcap. 8vo, half bound paper boards, **3s. 6d.**

" This is a dainty and pleasing little volume, to be prized by all devotees of the Muse."—*Daily Telegraph.*

THE COUNTESS KATHLEEN : A Dramatic Poem. By W. B. YEATS. Uniform with above.

" It is impossible to read these poems without falling under their fascination and taking them home to heart."—*Academy.*

IRISH FAIRY TALES. Edited by W. B. YEATS. Illustrated by JACK B. YEATES. (A volume of " The Children's Library.") Pinafore cloth binding, floral edges, **2s. 6d.**

" An exquisite collection . . . with an interesting preface by the author."—*Bookman.*

FINN AND HIS COMPANIONS. By STANDISH O'GRADY. Illustrated by J. B. YEATS. Uniform with above.

JOHN SHERMAN, AND DHOYA. By GAN-CONAGH. (Vol. X. of " Pseudonym Library.") Third edition. Paper, **1s. 6d.** ; cloth, **2s.**

" Clever as ' John Sherman ' is, cleverness seems almost an odious quality to ascribe to pathos so unassertive, humour so delicate, and observation so penetrative."—*Saturday Review.*

THE PARNELL MOVEMENT: Being the History of the Irish Question from the Death of O'Connell to the Suicide of Pigott. By T. P. O'CONNOR, M.P. Crown 8vo, cloth boards, **2s.**

" Able, readable, and full of force, and replete with information, it is, we believe, the best and most comprehensive work on the subject yet published."—*Nonconformist.*

LONDON :

T. FISHER UNWIN, PATERNOSTER SQUARE, E.C.

IRISH LITERATURE

THE AUTOBIOGRAPHY of THEOBALD

WOLFE TONE: A Chapter from Irish History,
1790–1798. Edited, with an Introduction, by R.
BARRY O'BRIEN, of the Middle Temple, Barrister-at-
Law, Author of "Fifty Years of Concessions to Ireland," "Thomas Drummond," &c. 2 vols., with
Photogravure Frontispiece to each. 4 Steel Plates,
and a Letter in facsimile. Royal 8vo, cloth, 32s.

"The book, entirely apart from any political question, is delightful
reading."—*Daily News.*

LIFE OF JOHN BOYLE O'REILLY.

Together with his Complete Poems and Speeches. By
JAMES JEFFREY ROCHE. Edited by Mrs. JOHN BOYLE
O'REILLY. With Introduction by H. E. JAMES
CARDINAL GIBBONS, Archbishop of Baltimore. Por-
traits and Illustrations. Royal 8vo, cloth, £1 1s.

DIARY of the PARNELL COMMISSION.

By JOHN MACDONALD, M.A. Revised, with Additions,
from the *Daily News.* Large crown 8vo, cloth, 6s.

IRELAND. By the Hon. EMILY LAWLESS,

Author of "Hurrish: A Study," &c. (Vol. X. of
"The Story of the Nations.") Maps and Illustrations.
Cloth, 5s.

THE NEED AND USE OF GETTING

IRISH LITERATURE INTO THE ENGLISH
TONGUE: An Address by the Rev. STOPFORD A.
BROOKE at the Inaugural Meeting of the Irish Literary
Society in London. Second Edition. Small 4to, paper
covers, 1s.

"A charming and suggestive piece of writing."—*Speaker.*

LONDON:

T. FISHER UNWIN, PATERNOSTER SQUARE, E.C.

THE STORY OF THE NATIONS.

Each Volume is furnished with Maps, Illustrations, and Index.

Large crown 8vo, fancy cloth, gold lettered, price **5s.** *each.*

A List of the Volumes.

Some Press Notices.

"That useful series."—*The Times.*

"An admirable series."—*Spectator.*

"The series is likely to be found indispensable in every school library."—*Pall Mall Gazette.*

Illustrated Catalogue of the Series, post free.

LONDON: T. FISHER UNWIN, PATERNOSTER SQUARE, E.C.

www.ingramcontent.com/pod-product-compliance
Lightning Source LLC
Chambersburg PA
CBHW020540270326
41927CB00006B/662